the
people
book

Muriel James is a Consultant in Human Relations and Communication to school systems, government agencies, and business, and a Vice President of the International Transactional Analysis Association. She received her doctorate in educational psychology from the University of California, Berkeley, and is former Director of the Oasis Alternate High School in Lafayette, California. Dr. James is an ordained minister and a licensed marriage and family counselor. She is a former faculty member of the University of California and California State University Extension divisions and of the California School of Professional Psychology.

Dorothy Jongeward is President of the Transactional Analysis Management Institute, Inc., in Pleasant Hill, California and Trustee of the International Transactional Analysis Association. She is a lecturer and consultant in the fields of psychology, family life education, careers and education for women. Her bachelor's degrees are in psychology and education. Her master's degree from Washington State University is in educational guidance. Ms. Jongeward is a life member of the California Marriage Counseling Association. She is a faculty member of the University of California Extension and former high school teacher of psychology, sociology, English, and family life education.

Muriel James and Dorothy Jongeward are co-authors of the best-selling book BORN TO WIN: *Transactional Analysis with Gestalt Experiments* (Addison-Wesley, 1971).

This book is in the Addison-Wesley INNOVATIVE SERIES.

ISBN-0-201-3279-1
DEFGHIJK-KP-810798

Muriel James
Dorothy Jongeward

the people book

transactional analysis for students

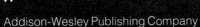

Addison-Wesley Publishing Company

Menlo Park, California   Reading, Massachusetts
London   Amsterdam   Don Mills, Ontario   Sydney

contents

introduction

The purpose of THE PEOPLE BOOK is to increase your understanding about people—yourself and others. It uses the theory and methods of Transactional Analysis to explain why you behave as you do, feel the way you feel, and say the things you say. It will also help you understand why some people act like winners, some act like losers, and why some go around in circles, neither winning nor losing, but just going nowhere. In addition, it will show you how to change what you want to change about your feelings and behavior and your relationships with other people, so that you can expand your winning streak.

The book is designed for individual or group study. Each unit begins with brief case studies followed by 1) theory directly related to the cases, 2) exercises for individual and group use, and 3) suggested research. Many exercises have been included so that you will have some options.

1 winners and losers

case study 1   From earliest childhood, Ellie's mother disliked her because she was homely. When she was six, her father, who was fond of her, was put in a sanatorium as an alcoholic. Despite wealth and social prestige, life with her mother and brothers was lonely and unhappy. This became worse when her parents and one brother died and, at age ten, she went to live with her grandmother, aunt, and uncles who had many problems of their own. Ellie's grandmother was disapproving and even stricter than her mother. Ellie, forced to wear odd clothes, was not permitted to have friends, and was made to wear a heavy steel brace because of poor posture. Although Ellie was very bright, her grandmother cared only that she be a social success and would not allow her to attend college.

case study 2   As a child, Goldie lived next to a police station where she often heard the tortures of political prisoners and worried that her politically active sister might be among them. Goldie's family escaped from the terror-ridden city and went to Milwaukee when she was eight. There Goldie worked long hours in a grocery store, yet for her school was so important that, at age ten, she organized and led a town meeting to raise money for books for children who could not afford them. When Goldie's mother insisted she drop out of school and only work, Goldie fled to Denver to live with her older sister so she could continue to study.

case study 3   Born to Jewish parents in an area where Jews were hated, Al was very slow in learning to talk. At school he was backward in his studies and in sports, and his father was ashamed of his lack of athletic ability. As a senior Al stayed out of school for six months with a nervous breakdown and one of his teachers claimed he'd never make a success of anything. Al, with no friends, lonely and shy, acquired odd mannerisms, made up his own religion, chanted hymns to himself, and was regarded even by his parents as very "different." He first failed the entrance exams to the university, and then repeated them successfully, but his record was not outstanding.

4

case study 4   Because Tom's head was large at birth, he was thought to have brain fever. During his first year in school, his teacher complained about his habit of dreaming, and suggested that he might be mentally ill. His mother didn't agree, so withdrew him from school and taught him at home. Throughout childhood, Tom continually experimented to find out how things were put together and how they worked. Neighbors accused him of being crazy, and the other children left him alone with his crazy games. Even his father thought he was a strange child. In all his life he received only three months of formal education.

case study 5   White children were forbidden to play with Martie. He was born in Georgia. The violence around him was so intolerable that he attempted suicide twice before the age of thirteen. Later he became a brilliant student, one of six blacks among a hundred whites. "I remember," he said, "once at an outing how worried I was when I found they were serving watermelon. I didn't want to be seen eating it because of the association in many people's minds between Negroes and watermelon. It was silly, I know, but it shows how white prejudices can affect a Negro."[1]

These brief case studies are of Eleanor Roosevelt, world-renowned humanitarian and political figure; Golda Meir, famed as Israel's second premier; Albert Einstein, genius in mathematics and famous for his theory on relativity; Thomas Edison, who invented, among other things, the electric light and the phonograph; and Martin Luther King, Jr., courageous civil rights leader.

They might have been expected to become losers; might have become physically destructive, delinquent, mentally ill, and retarded. Instead, each of them became a well-known winner, although their start in life looked bleak.

What does it mean to be a winner?

How do winners act?

And do winners ever lose?

Everyone is born to win. Winners sometimes lose, and they also make mistakes. But losers can be spotted as people who make the same mistakes over and over again. They don't seem to be able to learn from them.

Winners, on the other hand, do learn from their mistakes and seldom repeat the same ones. It's been said that losers are secretly afraid to win and don't know what to do with their success. In contrast, winners know what to do when they lose; they have alternate plans.

Between winners and losers there are the fifty percenters, who fall back two steps for every two they get ahead, just managing to stay even. Like people treading water, they keep afloat. Inevitably, when things go well for them, a number of things also seem to go badly. They tend to end up where they started out. These kinds of people are *nonwinners*.

Have you ever noticed how excited people get when they win something important or how depressed they get when they lose something important? Many people think of themselves as winners, losers, or nonwinners. For instance, an itinerant tramp was found dead in a drainage ditch with a tatoo on his arm that read, "Born to Lose." He thought of himself as a loser and apparently he was.

Everyone was born to be a winner but many people have such unhappy experiences that they begin to feel as if they can't quite make it. No one really wants to be a loser, yet many people really believe they were "born to lose" and may even set themselves up so they *will* lose. Others feel that they'll never quite make it and set themselves up so they don't. These feelings are expressed in words and actions. For example:

"I never have time to study" is a loser's excuse really meaning,
"I'm afraid to try, or studying is not important."

"I didn't think about it" is a loser's excuse really meaning,
"I'm not responsible" for getting pregnant, or for getting VD, or for getting in a car accident.

"Even if I could make it, I'll never get a chance" really means,
"Everyone's against me so I won't try."

"How could I have been so stupid" really means,
"It's not my fault, that's the way I am so I don't have to be responsible."

"I'll try to get it finished on time but probably I won't get it quite done," is a *nonwinner's* excuse. It means,
"I try a lot, but I better not succeed."

"I just can't ever get more than a C in math" is a *nonwinner's* excuse which means,
"The teacher doesn't like me, so why bother," or "I'm not good enough."

Often such statements reveal a basic attitude of I'm not-OK. People who use them constantly think of themselves as losers or nonwinners. They have not dared or learned how to take responsibility of achieving what they want to achieve. Instead, they might blame their clothes, intelligence, race, background, sex, physical characteristics, parents' occupation, religion, and so forth for their misfortunes.

Winners, in contrast to losers, seldom blame others for their mistakes, their faults, and their problems. Instead, they take responsibility for themselves because they feel basically OK. Some examples of what a winner might say:

"Well, I sure learned and I'll never make that mistake again."
Translated, this means, "It's not the end of the world if I make a mistake."

"If he (she) doesn't like me, maybe it's partly my fault." This really means, "I like myself and the other person well enough to want to figure out what we can do to straighten things out between us."

"This has been a tough week! Now I'm going to plan for some fun," meaning, "It's all right to take care of myself and it's OK to enjoy life."

"Maybe they haven't had as many chances as I have," indicates a winner's concern that it's important to try to understand less fortunate people, and that everyone is not alike.

Most people have times when they feel and act like winners—things are going well and they feel OK. But they may also have times when they feel and act like losers—things are going badly and they feel not-OK, or times when they're just treading water and things are just so-so. A tennis champion may feel like a loser on the dance floor. An award-winning dancer may feel like a loser when trying to compete in sports. An honors student may feel like a loser when trying to get a date. A student who's a popular date may feel like a loser when trying to make high grades.

Stop for a few minutes right now and think about yourself. In what situations do you think of yourself as a loser? as a winner? or as sort of so-so? When did you begin to think that way? Some of the things that may be said about winners:

They don't beat other people by winning over them and making them lose.

Winners respond authentically by being credible, trustworthy, responsive, and genuine, both as individuals and as members of society.

Few people are 100 percent winners. It's a matter of degree.

Winners have different potentials. Achievement is not the most important thing. Being real, honest, and open is.

Winners are not afraid to do their own thinking and to use their own knowledge. They can separate facts from opinion and don't pretend to have all the answers.

Winners don't play helpless nor do they play the blaming game. Instead, they assume responsibility for their own lives.

To winners, time is precious. They don't kill it. Rather, they know their past, are aware and alive in the present, and look forward to the future.

Winners can freely enjoy themselves. They can also postpone enjoyment.

Winners learn to know their feelings and their limitations and are not afraid of them.

Winners care about others.

winner and loser names

People draw winner/loser conclusions about themselves when they are very young. Experiences of all kinds affect people's attitudes about themselves. Words used to describe them by parents, brothers and sisters, friends, teachers or other significant people carry messages, as do the words that are used about them and those they may overhear.

People's identities are frequently tied in with their names. For example, a derogatory name or nickname or epithet may cause anxiety and loser feelings. A pleasant or popular name may contribute to winner feelings.

Parents give particular names to their children for many reasons. Biblical names such as David and Jonathan or Martha and Mary may be given by parents who want their children to reflect the characteristics associated with those names. The same is true for names from Greek mythology such as Jason and Ulysses; or if children are named after national heroes, fictional characters, popular movie stars, friends, or members of the family. In most cases there is some parental expectancy accompanying the name.

This expectancy may or may not be lived up to; but as children grow up, they continue to get winner and loser messages when their name is used. For example, a young man admonished with "John Timothy Adams!" may get a different message than when more softly called "Johnny." As Mark Twain wrote, "When a teacher calls a boy by his entire name, it means trouble."

Having a name is part of having an identity. Most people feel uncomfortable if their name is mispronounced or forgotten. Sometimes people dislike their name and decide to change it, either because of the associations it carries or because they've chosen to change and want to underline that fact with a new name of their own choice.

Many men use only their initials and surnames as identification. The term *Mr.* does not show whether or not the man is married, as do the terms *Miss* or *Mrs.* Most women take their husband's surname at marriage, but more and more prefer to keep their maiden name or be known as *Ms.* This is part of *their* identification. People retain or change their names for many reasons. The following case illustrates how one's name is part of one's identity.

As a youth, he was known as Hasanoanda of the Senecas. His real name was Donehogawa, Keeper of the Western Door of the Long House of the Iroquois. Donehogawa started work at age ten as a stable boy on an army post where he was so ridiculed for his poor use of English that he decided to do well in school to avoid being laughed at. Later he took the name of Ely Samuel Parker "because of the prejudice against Indian names and because he wanted to be taken seriously." He became military secretary to President Grant and was appointed

Commissioner of Indian Affairs. Parker's reforms saved the treasury millions of dollars and many lives because of his negotiating skills which he used to avoid another war on the Plains. His success created political enemies in Washington who constantly sniped at him and embarrassed him. Fearing he would do his people more harm than good, he resigned, made a fortune in New York City, and 'lived out his life as Donehogawa, Keeper of the Western Door of the Long House of the Iroquois."[2]

grandfather Cesar, grandson Cesar

Some people appear to have similar interests to their forefathers—especially if named after them. For example, Cesar Chavez, in his efforts to better living conditions for farm workers, shows a similar concern to that of his grandfather. Cesar was named after his grandfather, who had been a peon in Mexico and came to the United States as a homesteader. The grandfather was a strong and capable man, who was concerned with feeding any hungry strangers who happened by as well as his 15 children and many grandchildren. Cesar lived on his grandfather's farm until he was 10. Then, in the midst of the Depression, the grandfather died and the farm had to be sold for taxes. Cesar's parents started off in search of work. "Cesar grew up in one labor camp after another, where home might be a tarpaper shack or a tent, or between camps it might be the dry side of a highway bridge, where he crouched to stay out of the rain."[3] He attended over 30 schools, and reached the seventh grade still unable to read and write well.

He was always reminded that he was an alien, a foreigner. He wasn't allowed into "Anglo Town," where the white people lived. Once he tried to buy a hamburger in a diner that had a sign reading "Whites Only." The waitress laughed at him and threw him out, saying, "What's the matter, can't you read? Damn dumb Mex."[3]

Some people with these kinds of experiences might feel like losers. Cesar Chavez apparently didn't. He fought against the name-calling and, like his grandfather of the same name, has worked to provide more food for his people.

Names used publicly and privately often infer winner and loser meanings. Name-calling in public is common; so is the use of endearing names in private.

Nicknames, whether used privately or in public, can be compliments or put-downs. They are highly suggestive labels. Some nicknames conjure up physical images. Fatso, Stringbean, Freckles, Venus, Blondie, Piano-legs, Shortie, Fish-face, and Dimples all focus on appearance. Some nicknames imply behavioral characteristics: Stupid, Sweetie-pie, Monster, Knuckle-head, the Clod.

What's in a name? Sometimes a great deal. People's self-image, their winner and loser feelings, are often a response to what they were called as children.

summary

In summary, people become winners in spite of their names, in spite of negative pressures from society, poor family background, unhappy experiences, physical defects, or ill health.

Everyone is born a potential winner; becoming one is a matter of developing and using this potential.

exercises

1 about winners (group)

Discuss what you think a person who is a winner is like. What is it that makes a person a winner? List at least eight characteristics which can later be shared with the class.

2 about losers (group)

Discuss what you think a person who is a loser is like. What is it that makes a person a loser? List at least eight characteristics which can later be shared with the class.

Now select a spokesperson for your group who will report the decisions of the group to the entire class.

3 looking at me (individual)

This exercise is for personal growth.

☐ Think of five people whom you know well. List their names across the top of a sheet of paper.

☐ Under their names write what you think are their winner and loser characteristics.

☐ Next, try to imagine what each of them might write about you.

☐ If you would like them to think about you differently, what would you need to do?

4 you and your name (group)

In small groups discuss the following for 10-15 minutes:

☐ Where you got your name, who chose it, and what implications it had. (For example, if you were named after someone you probably were expected to be somewhat like that person. If so, why?)

☐ Your surname, where it came from and what cultural background it reflects. (For example, your name may have been shortened or changed by your parents or grandparents if they were immigrants. If so, why?)

5 new name experiment (group)

☐ As an experiment, think about what you might be like if you had a different name than you now have. Write it on a name tag or put it on a card in front of you.

☐ Next write down the adjectives that would describe the new you with the new name.

☐ Discuss this with others in your group. As you discuss your name, act, and speak according to the adjectives you selected.

suggested research

1 animal comparison

Think of yourself as an animal. If you were an animal what animal would you be?

☐ Find (or draw) a picture of this animal.

☐ List under it the traits that you see in yourself that this animal reminds you of.

☐ When you bring this in to the next class session, let the other group members guess what you chose. Find out if they see you the way you see yourself.

☐ Share your reasons for your selection.

☐ Guess at other people's choices and listen

to their reasons for their selections. Do they see themselves in a similar way to the way you see them?

2 winner and loser collages

☐ Go through magazines or newspaper articles you have around the house.

☐ Tear out pictures that show winner and loser characteristics.

☐ Bring them to school. During the first ten minutes of class paste your pictures on large sheets of paper for a collage.

☐ Put the collages on the wall and discuss your agreement and disagreement for no more than five minutes.

3 celebrity profile

☐ Select a well-known figure who is currently getting a lot of newspaper and/or magazine publicity.

☐ Collect a packet of news clippings about this person.

☐ Study them carefully and write a brief essay that focuses on the winning or losing characteristics that are reported.

4 family names

☐ Ask one or both of your parents to sit down and talk with you for a few minutes. Tell them that you want to understand the meaning of your name and ask them about where they got it and why they gave it to you.

☐ Then ask them about their names, whether they liked them or not when they were little, and how they feel about their names now.

5 thinking and feeling journal

Start a private journal of insights you have gained from this unit and continue making entries throughout the entire course. You may also want to use the journal for making notes on the exercises that occur at the end of each unit in this book. At the end of the course you will have a sketch of yourself and your behavior and also have a better understanding of other people.

2 introduction to ta

case study 1   Sandra constantly daydreamed of becoming a model, movie star, or airline hostess. Between classes, as she munched on a candy bar, she would gather with a group of friends and talk about Hollywood. Even though Sandra knew that having acne and being overweight would keep her from getting these jobs, she continued to eat things that weren't good for her.

case study 2   Cynthia was working for a music scholarship. She played the flute well and hoped for a place in a symphony orchestra after college. Her father was dead and her mother worked hard to support Cynthia and her three younger sisters. Early each school day Cynthia went to the neighbors' house where she cooked breakfast and fixed lunches for their children. In the afternoon she baby-sat for her sisters and did her homework. In the evening Cynthia practiced her flute, paying for her lessons with the money earned each morning. Friday and Saturday nights she had fun with her friends.

case study 3   Jerry seemingly had no goals. Each day was much like the day before. Jerry was into drugs pretty heavily and rarely stayed "clean." At school he often half slept through classes or withdrew into a fantasy world. There he saw himself as popular and successful. But in the real world Jerry had no close friends he thought he could trust and was generally considered a failure.

Sometime in your life you've probably wondered why you think, feel, and act the way you do—most people have. You've probably also wondered why your friends, parents, relatives, and teachers do some of the things they do.

Transactional Analysis is one way to figure out answers to some of these questions. It is a theory and a method of understanding how people communicate with each other and where they seem to be going with their lives.

People have problems. Transactional Analysis is one tool which can be used to help understand these problems and solve them. Transactional Analysis (often called TA) helps people set goals for themselves and sometimes even to discover potentials they didn't know they had. By learning to understand its principles many people learn how to direct their lives so that they can be more of the winners they were meant to be.

TA consists of four different kinds of analysis: structural analysis, transactional analysis, games analysis, and script analysis.

structural analysis

Structural analysis is the analysis of an individual personality. It helps people understand who they are and how they got that way. In other words, structural analysis is about what makes people tick.

Of course people are different. They differ in looks, actions, feelings, and the expectations they have for themselves. But why? Is it because they come from different parts of the country, from different social and ethnic backgrounds? have different kinds of childhoods? have different parents? different abilities? different experiences and training? Why are people different?

Structural analysis gives one answer to this question by using the idea of three ego states—Parent, Adult, and Child—to explain how we act and feel because of these three parts of our personalities.

It helps people to understand the impact of their parent figures on their own personalities, an impact they often are not aware of. It helps them to understand more fully how the things that happened in childhood affect them now. In addition, it teaches them how to think, and how to change things they may not like about themselves, and how to strengthen those things they do like.

transactional analysis

Transactional analysis (proper) is the second form of analysis. It explains how we related to other people—the kinds of transactions that go on between us. It explains why some transactions (words and actions) communicate effectively, and why other transactions lead to misunderstandings and cut people off from each other; why some transactions are open and straight, and others closed and defensive or phoney and crooked.

TA helps us figure out what is going on when, for instance, the Parent part of one person relates to or transacts with the Child part of another person; and why transactions look, sound, and feel good or bad.

games analysis

Games analysis is the third method by which to understand how people interact. Psychological games always have a hidden message underneath the actual words that are said. Games analysis is concerned with figuring out what the hidden message is, why it is being given, and what the person gets out of sending it. What he or she gets is usually a feeling of being victimized, or of rescuing or persecuting someone. In other words, in psychological games, people act out the roles of Victims, Rescuers, or Persecutors, playing parts rather than being themselves. As Shakespeare wrote, "All the world's a stage and all the men and women merely players."

As an example of psychological game playing, sometimes people seem to invite criticism. It's as though they *want* put-downs. Sometimes they look for ways to put others down and persecute them. Sometimes they like to feel that they can solve the problems of others and rescue them, even if people don't really want it.

Games are played to manipulate people and somebody usually ends up feeling bad. Why would one do things to make oneself or others feel bad?

Is there an advantage in playing games instead of being real with each other? Games analysis helps us to figure these questions out.

script analysis

The fourth kind of analysis is script analysis. A person's script is the life plan that he or she lives by, usually without being aware of it. A life plan is programed into the brain. It develops from the messages and experiences one has as a child. Like a theatrical script, this psychological script has action, a plot, dialogue, characters, and scenery.

Different people have different scripts. Some people act as though they're bent for destruction. Still others just go around in circles, going nowhere. Others develop and grow all their lives. Why is that so?

Script analysis helps us to discover what our script is and how we got it and how we can change what we want to change.

origin of transactional analysis

Originally psychotherapists used TA to help disturbed people get over personal problems. However, the basic ideas were so useful that many other people found ways to apply it to their daily lives.

Business men and women discovered that TA helped them at work; families used it at home; hospital staffs applied it to their work; prison inmates discovered that they could change their lives by using it; government agencies discovered TA as an aid to communication; teachers found they could teach better if they were TA trained; and now, many students have discovered its value.

The theory of Transactional Analysis was developed by a psychiatrist, Dr. Eric Berne. Dr. Berne wrote that the idea emerged when he was treating a successful court-room lawyer of high repute.

"[He] raised his family decently, did useful community work, and was popular socially. But in treatment he often did have the attitude of a little boy. Sometimes during the hour he would ask: 'Are you talking to the lawyer or to the little boy?' When he was away from his office or the court-room, the little boy was very apt to take over. He would retire to a cabin in the mountains away from his family, where he kept a supply of whiskey, morphine, lewd pictures, and guns. There he would indulge in child-like fantasies, fantasies he had had as a little boy, and the kinds of sexual activity which are commonly labeled 'infantile'."[4]

Dr. Berne was struck by his client's different attitudes toward money—miserly, rational, and generous—and concluded that these attitudes could be traced to three different aspects of his personality, which he called the Parent, Adult, and Child ego states.

The client's benevolent behavior was copied from his philanthropist father, and he was generous when he acted from his Parent ego state. His rational behavior was from his Adult, who processed information intelligently. His miserly behavior, which included petty theft, came from his Child ego state. In that state he felt and acted the same way he had acted when he was a little boy.

Naturally, this man's wife and teenage children were confused and resentful about these transactions.

summary In summary, you can put the tools of TA—structural analysis, transactional analysis proper, games analysis, and script analysis—to work for you. Just as Dr. Berne was able to help his client understand himself better and make positive changes, TA is a practical way to evaluate behavior and change what needs to be changed.

exercises

1 evaluating case studies (group or individual)

Review the case studies at the beginning of the unit (page 12) and answer the following questions:

☐ How realistic is Sandra's goal to become a stewardess?

☐ Is Cynthia likely to reach her goal?

☐ What do you think and feel about the way she works on her goals?

☐ Do you suppose Jerry feels most often like a Victim, a Persecutor, or a Rescuer?

☐ What role might other people who know him see him playing?

2 beginning to know your ego states (group)

Each of the four methods for analyzing people and their transactions will be presented in detail in later chapters. However, the following four exercises will introduce you to the basic concepts.

Imagine you are at home alone. The doorbell rings unexpectedly. A mailman hands you an envelope with a letter saying you've held the winning ticket and just won a new car.

☐ What are your feelings and thoughts? What would you do?

☐ How would you have felt as a child? Do you feel this now?

☐ What might each of your parents do in this situation? Would your behavior resemble that of one of your parent figures?

☐ What do you think is the most rational thing to do?

3 beginning to know your transactions (group)

Discuss a transaction that you've observed in the last three days in which you felt the people understood each other.

☐ Why do you think this transaction was successful?

Discuss a transaction you observed in which you thought the people misunderstood each other or left feeling bad.

☐ Why do you think this transaction was unsuccessful?

☐ Discuss a situation where you felt like a Victim (e.g., your parents wouldn't let you borrow the car) and then switched behavior and acted like a Persecutor to your parents by acting sulky or abusive.

4 beginning to spot a game (group)

☐ Discuss a situation where you tried to be a Rescuer to someone by helping them out, but they turned down your help so you ended up feeling like a Victim.

5 beginning to know your script (group)

Most people are not aware of living out a life plan that follows a script. To begin to know yours, think about yourself for a few minutes then discuss the following:

☐ What happens to people like me who _____? Supply phrases such as: studies hard, or never studies, is always on time, always late, or eats nourishing foods or lives on hamburgers and cokes.

16

☐ Then discuss, "If I go on doing _____ as I now do, what will be the logical consequence?

☐ Next discuss, "If I go on always feeling _____ as I now feel, how will I end up?

suggested research

1 winners and losers in daily life

Look up examples in any news magazine that illustrate:

☐ A person suddenly changing behavior. This is likely to involve a change of ego states.

☐ Transactions between people which seem to be satisfying or unsatisfying.

☐ Someone who is acting like a Victim, Persecutor, or Rescuer when circumstances don't justify their roles.

☐ Someone whose behavior seems to indicate that he or she is acting in predictable ways which may be part of their script.

☐ Bring these examples to class and discuss them.

2 your shoe box

Prepare a shoe box to bring to class. Fill it with things that somehow relate to your personality and tell something about you. Keep what's in your shoe box a secret until your teacher tells you what to do with it in class.

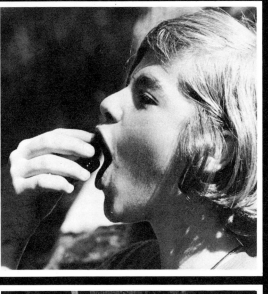

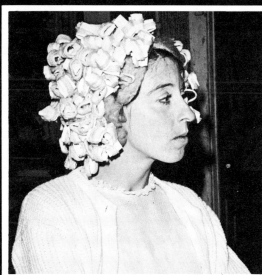

3 overview of personality structure

case study 1   Paul had just had an argument with his wife. His face was red and his voice was shrill. He was in their room pounding his fist in his palm when the phone rang. It was his boss. As Paul talked to his boss, his facial expression, tone of voice, and whole demeanor seemed to change immediately. He could be heard repeating calmly, "OK, I'll be at work tomorrow a half hour early. Thanks for calling."

case study 2   Audrey acted very dependent. For example, at school she usually checked several times with her friends to see if she understood her assignment correctly. She spoke in a small whispery voice much of the time and cried easily. She acted the same way at home. However, when her father was disabled and her mother took a full-time job for the first time, Audrey's behavior changed at home. Each day after school she tended to her younger brother, straightened up the house, started dinner, and set the table. When Audrey's mother came home from a long day as a grocery clerk, she would flop down in a big chair, take off her shoes, and heave a deep sigh. Audrey would bring her a cup of tea, pat her on the shoulder, and say something like, "Don't worry, Mom, it's going to be all right." Audrey's new behavior with her mother was very similar to the way her mother had treated her, when Audrey came home from school very tired.

case study 3   Susan transferred to City High School in the middle of her sophomore year. She had lived on a farm in another state most of her life and had been popular in her previous school. However, at City High Susan was very uncomfortable. Her accent showed that she came from a different part of the country. Sometimes Susan didn't want to talk for fear that she would say "you all" and be laughed at. One day she and her mother sat down, talked the whole situation over, and developed a plan. The plan was that Susan would carefully observe students in her classes, think of five she might like to be friends with, and figure out what she would need to do to win their friendship. Within a month, Susan had friends.

Have you ever noticed how everybody changes behavior from time to time? How sometimes people act as though they had logically figured things out? How sometimes they act impulsively as though they hadn't thought about it? Or how they comply as though they were puppets on a string? Or put things off, as though they can't make up their own minds? Have you noticed that sometimes people act in a caring way? Sometimes in a domineering and critical way? If you have, you've noticed their using different ego states. Different ways of behaving are common to people of every age and every culture. It is not surprising, then, that a happy smile or tantrum may remind you of a child and a critical frown or warm hug may remind you of some parent figure.

introduction to structural analysis

Structural analysis is based on the theory that everyone's personality consists of a Child, an Adult, and one or more Parents. These three parts of personality are called ego states—the Parent ego state, the Adult ego state, and the Child ego state. When capitalized in this book, these words will refer to parts of the personality. When not capitalized, these words will refer to people.

The structure of personality can be diagramed. For convenience the capital letters *P-A-C* are used to represent the ego states.

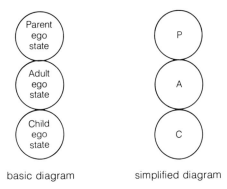

basic diagram   simplified diagram

Parent ego state

The Parent ego state contains the attitudes and behavior that are observed and copied from significant parent figures. Sometimes the behavior from a Parent ego state is prejudicial and critical. Sometimes it may be caring, affectionate, and protective. In the Parent ego state we act out behavior copied from the actual parent figures.

For example, a person whose parent is prejudiced against people of a different race, religion, education background, and so forth, may discover he or she is similarly prejudiced. A person whose parent likes to give advice, or who likes to take care of people in distress may find him /herself using similar behavior.

21

When you are acting as your parent figures used to act, you are in your Parent ego state. Each person has different parent figures; therefore, each person has a Parent ego state that is different from anyone else's.

Adult ego state   The Adult ego state is not related to a person's age. Rather, it refers to the ability to think rationally on the basis of objective facts. For example, if you gather information about your negative Parent behavior and decide to change it, the change occurs through the Adult ego state.

When you are gathering facts, organizing them, and making decisions on the basis of facts, you are in your Adult ego state. When you are objectively giving other people information you are also in your Adult. When you are reading a book, doing your math, or planning a project, again you are mainly using your Adult ego state.

Child ego state   The Child ego state contains all the impulses a person was born with. Each infant has needs, feelings, the desire to explore and grow. Each infant learns how best to have these needs met, often by manipulation. The Child ego state also contains "recordings" of childhood training and experiences. These experiences affect our later behavior. For example, if one is scared in childhood by a large mean dog, that person is likely to feel panic in the Child ego state at the sight of a large dog coming close even if past childhood. If someone has a large dog as a friendly childhood pet, that person, when grown, is likely to trust dogs easily.

As another example, if a person is humiliated by other students or by the teacher on the first day of kindergarten or first grade, he or she is likely to feel embarrassed or anxious when starting a new class even if it's eight years later in high school.

On the other hand, if a person makes friends and feels liked by the teacher on the first day of school, that person will tend to have more confidence when entering a new class later in life.

summary   When people feel and act as they did when in childhood, they are in their Child ego state. When they copy their parents' attitudes and behavior, they are in their Parent ego state. When they are acting rationally, they are in their Adult ego state.

exercises

1 evaluating case studies (group or individual)

Reread the case studies at the beginning of the unit (page 20) and answer the following questions:

- Which ego state was Paul in when arguing with his wife? Why do you think this?

- Which ego state was Paul in when talking with his boss? Why do you think this?

- Which ego state did Audrey use with her mother when her mother was tired? Why do you think that?

- Do you think it was effective? Why or why not?

- Which ego state was Susan in when she first came to City High?

- Which ego state did she use and how did she use it to gain friends?

2 your shoe box revealed

Do not let others know which is your box but turn it in to a committee or teacher who will redistribute the boxes to other people.

Each person in the class will then have someone else's box.

- On the basis of what's in the box, guess whose it is, write the person's name on a paper, and pass the box to someone else to do the same.

- After three or four people have guessed at who the owner is, the owner can then own up.

Discuss in small groups why the items were chosen and what they represent.

3 ego state reaction quiz (individual and group)

First, work on the quiz individually. After you do this, share your ideas in small groups.

On the quiz, identify each reaction as Parent, Adult, or Child (P, A, or C). These will be educated guesses, since you can't hear the tone of voice or see the gestures.

- A teacher drops her purse in the hall. A roll of quarters falls out, the paper breaks, and the quarters roll down the hall.
  1. If I step on a quarter and stand there a while, she'll probably go away.
  2. She should hang on to her purse better.
  3. I wonder why she has the roll of quarters.

- It's a competitive exam. You are competing with others for a big prize. Suddenly you observe your neighbor copying answers written on the inside of his hand.
  1. He should be ashamed of himself.
  2. That may affect my chances of winning.
  3. If I report it, he'll probably beat me up.

- A mimeograph machine in the business class, or a piece of equipment in the auto shop, breaks down.
  1. Wow! I don't know what to do about this mess.
  2. If I ever find out who tampered with this, I'll show them a thing or two.
  3. We'll need to get this repaired as soon as possible.

- A teacher is not satisfied with a book report.
  1. If I've told you once, I've told you a hundred times how to write it.

2. If you read the instructions you will be able to do your report accurately.

3. Why don't you try harder when I'm trying so hard to help you?

□ A student is not satisfied with a grade.

1. Gee, I just can't seem to understand. I'm so confused.

2. Is there anything I can do to pull up my grade?

3. You should have explained better.

4 various ego state responses (group)

In small groups figure out how one person might feel or respond in three different ways (three different ego states) to the same thing:

□ For example, a piece of chocolate cake:

P — Don't eat before dinner.

A — This piece of cake has at least 500 calories.

C — Wow, that looks good!

□ Smoke seeping under a door.

□ The sudden fainting of a teacher.

□ The knocking of a typewriter off a desk.

□ An unexpected compliment from the principal.

□ Now make up two common situations that students often face.

suggested research

1 imagining ego states of others

Imagine you are a school custodian who has just discovered a student taking money from a teacher's desk.

□ Write about the possible reaction of your three ego states.

Imagine you are a student who has just discovered a custodian taking money from the principal's office.

□ Write about the possible reactions of your three ego states.

  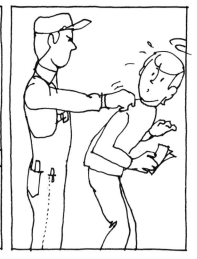

2 letting out your creative Child

Write a short poem or limerick of three stanzas
that illustrates each ego state. It doesn't have
to be perfect (the example that follows isn't),
just understandable.

One Parent I know is a bore.
    It constantly says, "Shut the
    door".
    If I do not comply, or say "no"
    with my eye
    The Parent says "Do it" and
    "Do it" and "Do it" and "Do it"
    and "Do it" and "Do it" some
    more.

My Adult I also can use.
    It thinks, and without a short
    fuse.
    It processes facts, finds out
    what it lacks
    With the skill of a poet or
    muse.

The Child's the fun part of me.
    It's creative as now you can
    see.
    But if it is crossed, by a cop on
    a horse
    It's likely to panic and flee.
    Flee, fly, flow, flum, Ho hum!

Or, if you don't want to write, draw a picture
illustrating the three ego states. Once again, it
doesn't have to be perfect, just understandable.

4 the Parent ego state

case study 1   Joe was president of the Spanish club. Although several students joined with enthusiasm at the beginning of the term, they quickly dropped out. Those who remained in the club always agreed with what Joe told them to do. He always set the date, hour, and agenda for the club. Joe's style of leadership was to tell others what they "should" do. He often stood and shook his finger at other club members reprovingly.

case study 2   Helen and her best friend, Loretta, were getting things out of their adjoining lockers when something fell to the concrete floor and scattered in small pieces down the hall. It was a lovely piece of pottery Loretta had worked hard on for a Mother's Day gift and it was smashed. Loretta's eyes filled with tears. Her friend Helen responded by putting her arm around her and saying, "Now don't worry. We'll figure something else out for your Mom."

case study 3   Lowell stood up to give a speech. His hands were shaking, his heart beat wildly, and he blushed a little. After taking a deep breath, Lowell straightened himself up, looked at the audience, and began to deliver his talk with confidence.

case study 4   Martha made many friends, but they were often unhappy with her. She was very bossy and frequently spoke in a high-pitched, shrill voice. She passed judgment on how her friends should behave, how they should dress, and even what they should eat. She was very critical of people outside "her group". While she was bright and often fun, her friends were often put off by her behavior.

development of the
Parent ego state   Children watch their parents and without realizing it, start to copy their behavior. They may act the Critical Parent and scold their pets, dolls, or younger brothers and

sisters as their mother or father scolds them. They may also act the Nurturing Parent, expressing affection as they observe their parents doing.

This process is called *incorporation*. Incorporation happens when a child absorbs the personality of one or more parent figures. Significant parent figures are not always the actual, biological parents. They may be step-parents, grandparents, baby-sitters, older brothers and sisters, and so forth.

For example, if a girl has a mother figure who works hard preparing the Thanksgiving feast for a large family gathering, the girl is likely to do the same thing when she grows up if she's in her Parent ego state. If a girl has a mother figure who doesn't like cooking for large gatherings and who prefers a restaurant on Thanksgiving, the girl, when she is grown up, may expect to do the same thing.

If a boy has a father figure who works very hard but has little time for fun, that boy may value hard work and seldom play when he is older. If a boy has a father figure who doesn't work hard but knows how to enjoy recreation, the boy has a model to copy when he is older.

parents and their ego states

One of the interesting things about parents is that *they* also have three ego states. Each parent figure has a Parent, Adult, and Child. Parents sometimes act like *their* parents. They also act and feel the way they did when they were children, as well as like thinking adults. Therefore, when children incorporate their parent figures, they incorporate their various ego states.

This means that, without knowing it, a person may copy all or part of their parent figures' personalities. Sometimes you may even act like a great-grandparent you never met! For example, like his or her father, a person may:

enjoy playing ball (like father's Child)

excel in math (like father's Adult)

be comforting when people are sick (like father's Parent)

People who incorporate their mother and father have a Parent ego state that can be diagramed as:

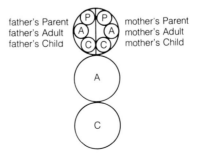

father's Parent   mother's Parent
father's Adult   mother's Adult
father's Child   mother's Child

People who incorporate other parent figures have a different Parent ego state. For example, someone reared by a mother, aunt, and older sister would have a Parent ego state containing each of them, as diagramed below left.

Someone who is partially reared by a grandparent and who has a regular baby-sitter would have a Parent ego state that would be diagramed as shown at right.

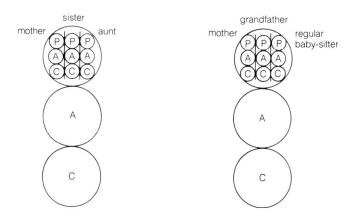

The attitudes, traditions, and prejudices of any culture and subculture are passed on from generation to generation through the Parent ego states. Even the way a person cooks can be parent-programed and go back many generations.

A bride served baked ham, and her husband asked why she cut the ends off. "Well, that's the way mother always did it," she replied. The next time his mother-in-law stopped by, he asked her why she cut the ends off the ham. "That's the way *my* mother did it," she replied. And when Grandma visited, she too was asked why she sliced the ends off. She said, "That's the only way I could get it into the pan!"

the outer and inner use of the Parent ego state

When people speak, make gestures, use a tone of voice, express an opinion, or give advice like any one of their parent figures, they are acting outwardly from their Parent ego state. Although they may not be aware of it, others can spot it. From their Parent ego states people can transact with any of the ego states in another person. This would be diagramed as:

For example, Harry from his Parent ego state may talk to all three ego states in Carolyn.

P → P   Carolyn, did you see those creeps that registered this morning?

P → A   Don't you think it's a waste of money for you to go to college, Carolyn. After all, you're just going to get married.

P → C   Carolyn, I don't think you should stay out so late. You look too tired.

In addition to copying their parents' behavior externally, people also are affected by their Parent ego state internally. They continue to hear the verbal "do this" and "don't do that" messages that their parents gave them years ago. They see again, like flashes of moving pictures, their parents' approving or disapproving facial expressions and behavior.

Like a videotape, these verbal and nonverbal messages are replayed and listened to inwardly by the Child. This can be diagramed as shown at left.

For example, when going into a store a person's Child might very much want a new record but not have money to pay for it.

If he or she had a parent who used to say, "You only live once, get everything you can," this person may feel "entitled" to walk out with the record without paying.

If he or she had a parent who used to say, "Whatever you do, don't get caught," this person may carefully steal the record and get away with it. In both these cases someone else gets hurt because of parental attitudes.

If she or he had a parent who used to say, "Don't take things that don't belong to you. Respect other people's property," this person may leave the store without the record.

summary   In summary, people copy their parents' behavior without realizing it. Most parents want the best for their children; sometimes they don't know how to give the best, sometimes they do. With TA awareness people can make a deliberate decision as to which behavior is OK to use and which is not. Parents are not perfect even though many children wish their's were. Understanding why one's parents are the way they are with all their imperfections is a tool winners use to feel good about themselves.

exercises

1 evaluating case studies (group or individual)

Review the case studies at the beginning of the unit (page 26) and answer the following questions:

☐ Which ego state did Joe use as president?

☐ Do you think he was effective?

☐ Which ego state was Loretta probably experiencing when the pottery dropped?

☐ Which ego state did Helen use in responding to Loretta?

☐ Which ego state was Lowell using at first?

☐ What do you think he might have heard from his Parent in his head that helped him switch behavior?

☐ Which ego state did Martha seem to be using a great deal with her friends?

2 Parent ego state vocabulary and body language (group)

Ego states can be identified if you listen to the words a person uses and the tone of voice, observe body language, facial expressions, and postures. Tune into these nonverbal clues and make lists according to what you have observed as typical Parent behavior.

Parent words or phrases (i.e., should, must)	*Parent* gestures, postures, facial expressions, tone of voice
_____	_____
_____	_____
_____	_____

3 parental opinions (group)

In small groups of six discuss the kinds of things parents say about the following:

getting an education	borrowing money
choosing a career	going to church
using drugs	doing homework
being a success	getting a job

4 parents' chat (group)

Now go into pairs and actually take the part of one of your parents. Speak and act as *they* would. Discuss one or two of the following:

☐ How you should behave on a date

☐ What their hopes are for you

☐ The masculine or feminine roles they expect you to fill

suggested research

1 using your imagination

Imagine you are walking down the street and you suddenly see an accident. A car is pulled over to the side, and a person is lying motionless.

☐ What do you think you would do? Take a minute to jot it down.

☐ Now look at what you just wrote.

☐ Ask yourself, "Was my response similar to the probable response of any of my parent figures?"

30

□ If it was, then it is logical to assume that you were using your Parent ego state in that particular situation.

Imagine you are taking care of a two-year-old child who accidently breaks one of his mother's most beautiful dishes.

□ What is your response to this child?

□ Is this response similar to what any of your parent figures would do?

□ If it is, you would be acting from your Parent ego state.

Imagine that your *favorite* teacher walks into the classroom, sits down, puts her head down on her hands, looking very depressed.

□ What do you think you might do? Write down a couple of sentences.

□ Now look at what you've written and try to figure out whether any of your parent figures would have done the same thing.

Next, imagine that a teacher you *dislike intensely* walks into the room, puts her head down on the desk, looking very depressed.

□ Write down in a few sentences what you might do.

□ Now look at your sentences and see if by any chance it's what any of your parent figures would do.

2 Parent behavior on television

□ Select one well-known TV show.

□ Watch for behavior that seems to come from the Parent ego state.

□ List positive and negative uses of the Parent.

5 the Adult ego state

case study 1   Chet Brownlee was chief custodian. He worked hard with his hands and thoughtfully with his brain when supervising other custodial staff. On the job he was considered to be both responsible and fair. After work, Chet's usual pattern was to go home, slump down in his favorite chair and take a catnap. His wife and children knew that "that's the time to leave Dad alone." After dinner he was often willing to help with the dishes and homework.

case study 2   Doug was a junior. His grades throughout high school were mediocre and he had no plans beyond graduation. He told his counselor he guessed maybe he'd get a job of some kind or another someday. The counselor offered him materials to read about possible vocations and also showed him what courses and grades he would need if he decided he'd go to college. Doug said he wasn't interested in the future.

case study 3   Juanita wanted to be a doctor and knew she had to get good grades to be accepted in medical school. She always expressed concern when others were unhappy. When her best friend's mother became alcoholic, Juanita began to spend much time on the phone every day trying to cheer up her friend. Although Juanita's school work had been superior, she fell behind in her studies and her grades dropped. After getting a poor report card, she decided to limit her time on the phone to 15 minutes a day.

case study 4   Jim and Ginny were going steady and often talked about getting married. One day when sitting around with a group of friends somebody suggested that they elope the day after graduation. "Wow, wouldn't that be great!" said Ginny. "It sure would," Jim added, "but then what? We'd have to live off our parents or go on welfare. I think we both need to have jobs for a while and get some experience before settling down."

introduction to the Adult ego state

Do you know that anyone can think clearly and rationally unless there is very severe brain damage? Thinking clearly is a function of the Adult ego state, but it is not related to being 18 years of age or older. The ability to think clearly begins to develop in early childhood, and it continues throughout life, if we don't sabotage it.

The Adult ego state gathers information, processes the information, and stores it on the basis of previous experiences. In processing information, the Adult estimates probabilities as a basis for action. A simple example of this would be a person getting up in the morning, looking out at an overcast sky, noting that the barometer has dropped, and estimating (guessing) that it's probably going to rain.

When you gather information in your Adult ego state, you use different sources. Each of these sources is important. First there is the external world—the world of facts and figures, objects and people—the world that can be objectively observed. Second is the inner world—the world of feelings and fantasies, prejudices and opinions—the inner world of the Parent and Child that can be known and managed by the Adult. Winners develop the ability to use both sources constructively. Gathering data and processing the information can be diagramed as shown at left.

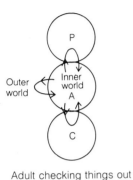

Adult checking things out

the Adult ego state and education

The Adult ego state is very much affected by a person's education. The more factual information you have about any subject—the more input the Adult has—the better the decisions made around that subject are likely to be.

Adult ego states vary among people partly because of the kind and amount of information they have gathered or been exposed to. A child brought up on a farm acquires lots of information about soil, climate, growing seasons, and animals. But that person, when grown up, may feel incompetent trying to get around on public transportation in a large city. A city child, when grown up, may be very knowledgable and confident about getting around in cities but be ignorant about how things grow.

In our culture, a child deprived of books, newspapers, and stimulating conversation will simply not have as well-informed an Adult ego state as people who have had these advantages.

Much of the material you are expected to learn in school may seem irrelevant to you because it is stored, rather than used immediately. For example, some students take algebra knowing that they are going into chemistry in college. Others may take it as a college entrance requirement not knowing what it might be used for in the future. It's hard to predict what information, stored now, will be of use in later life.

The more accurate the information is that people have about a certain subject, the more likely they are to make rational decisions about it. For example, many people have a lot of inaccurate information on sexuality, job requirements, married life, cost of living, and so forth. They may even have inaccurate information about themselves.

One purpose of this book is to help you know yourself better. In TA language this means your Adult learns more about your Parent and Child ego states. With new awareness, you will discover more of your winning potential.

the outer and inner use of the Adult ego state

People are able to act and speak from their Adults. For example, taking notes from a history book, giving a demonstration on how to repair faulty carburetors, totaling up a shopping list, or asking for directions are activities which involve mainly an Adult ego state.

Inward use of the Adult ego state may not be as observable. A person may appear to be daydreaming when actually trying to solve a problem as, for instance, what to wear to school. The inner Child may want to go barefooted. The inner Parent may say "That's not the proper dress for school". The inner Adult may know that there is a lot of broken glass in the yard. Without others' noticing what's going on, one is deciding what's practical to do (Adult), what one should do (Parent), or wants to do (Child). Any ego state could win the inner argument.

In addition to experiencing the dialogue inside our heads, people also listen with their Adults.

You have probably had the experience of hearing an assignment, knowing what the teacher wanted, and how you could get the information. You may also have had the opposite experience, when you were given an assignment and forgot it or felt confused about what your teacher really wanted. In the first situation, it was your Adult that was listening, in charge of your personality, and computing objectively. In the second situation, your Child may have been most active. For example, you could have been having a fantasy about being somewhere else and having fun, or feeling bad about having last night's argument with a good friend. Consequently your Adult was tuned out and you may not have heard what your teacher was saying.

The same situation also holds true for your teacher, friend, or parents. You give them some clear information, but they may not really hear it because they too listen from their Child or Parent ego states and are not on the same wavelength as you.

summary

In summary, everyone has problems, but regardless of how big a problem is, anyone can learn to solve it. Most things can be changed. Even if a problem is really tough, like having a physical handicap, or seems hopeless, a person can learn to cope by using the Adult.

Although everyone has an Adult ego state, some people do not use it often enough. Like a muscle which needs to be exercised in harmony with other muscles to function at its best, the Adult ego state also needs to be used. Unless it is, the Parent or Child ego states will take over.

exercises

1 evaluating case studies (group or individual)

Review the case studies at the beginning of the unit (page 32), and answer the following questions:

☐ Which ego state was Mr. Brownlee, the custodian, in at work? at home?

☐ Which ego states seemed most active in the counselor? in Doug?

☐ How was Juanita using each of her ego states?

☐ How was Juanita's Adult activated?

☐ How might Jim and Ginny have used each of their ego states during their relationship?

☐ Which ego state did Jim and Ginny each seem to use when discussing marriage with their friends?

2 Adult ego state vocabulary and body language (group)

Ego states can be identified if you listen to the words a person uses and the tone of voice, observe body language, facial expressions, and postures. Tune in to these nonverbal clues and make lists according to what you have observed as typical Adult behavior.

Adult words or phrases (i.e., is probably, the facts show)	*Adult* gestures, postures, facial expressions, tone of voice
_____	_____
_____	_____
_____	_____

3 animals' ego states (group)

Your teacher will show you a film on animals, if available. If a film is unavailable draw on your own experiences with pets or trips to the zoo or farm animals you've seen. During the film observe the animals' behavior for gestures and mannerisms which may reflect either Parent, Adult, or Child behavior. Watch for:

☐ Caring, disciplining, guiding the young

☐ Using an object as a tool to get food

☐ Playfulness, rage, curiosity, etc.

After the film go into small groups to compare notes. Discuss:

☐ The behavior you observed which seemed similar to Parent, Adult, and Child ego states

☐ Discuss the similarities or differences of the animals to human beings.

4 group problem solving

In small groups of six select a school problem that concerns the people in your group.

☐ One half of the group will give opinions about the problem from the Parent ego state.

☐ One half of the group will give the facts (Adult) they have about the problem.

☐ Staying in these ego states, debate the issue for 15 minutes, at which time you will need to have come to some conclusions.

☐ During the process identify a Child ego state if it gets into the act.

suggested research

1 Adult problem solving

☐ Think of a personal problem that you would like to solve.

☐ Write it down.

☐ List what each of your parent figures would say and do about the problem and how your Child ego state feels about the problem.

One parent figures' words and action	Another parent figures' words and action
_____	_____
_____	_____
_____	_____

My Child ego state feelings	Information my Adult has
_____	_____
_____	_____
_____	_____

☐ Next list what information you may still need before you make a decision.

☐ Figure out how to get this information.

☐ Now list the practical steps you need to take to solve this problem.

2 ads and the Adult
Choose some ads from a popular magazine that appeal to you and some that do not.

☐ Which ego state is the ad coming from?

☐ Which of your ego states does it appeal to?

☐ What are some of the cues that tell you you are in that ego state?

☐ Which ego state does your Adult think people use most of the time when they are buying products?

6   the Child ego state

case study 1   When Mike was almost five years old, his father died. He was too little to understand what had happened and felt hurt that his daddy had gone away and left him. At seventeen Mike had a hard time trusting men. He often complained, "The coach always leaves me when I need help." Other people thought that the coach gave Mike plenty of attention.

case study 2   When Karen was a little girl, she could get her father to do almost anything she wanted. She would snuggle against him and look up at him with wide eyes and a broad smile. As a high school student, she sometimes reverted to the same technique when she wanted to wheedle a special favor from a male teacher or student. This behavior was often resented and she was, on occasion, accused of having to flirt to get her way. Later she was fired from several jobs by bosses who said they were fed up with her trying to manipulate them.

case study 3   As a child, Carlos spent long hours alone. His parents argued a lot and it bothered him. Since he lived in the country, he retreated to a favorite spot on a hill and spent hours watching the clouds and making mental pictures out of them. At sixteen Carlos spent much of his school time gazing out the window. If a teacher raised his or her voice, Carlos wanted to leave. In discussions with friends he would tune out when the argument became heated.

case study 4   Sally liked to play with toys that rolled fast or that could be used to build things. She constantly heard things like, "Little girls don't play with such toys", "Sally is such a tomboy!", "Sally just doesn't seem to know she's a girl." In high school Sally wanted to take math to prepare for an engineering course in college. She had no encouragement except from her math teacher and finally gave up her plans.

introduction to the Child ego state

Do you know people who, even though grown up, still like to roll down a hillside, run against the wind, enjoy the color and fragrance of flowers, giggle and be playful or silly? Or stamp their feet in a fit of temper, knock their fist through a wall, pout, stick out their tongues, withdraw in silence, obey or rebel against authority without thinking? If so, you have seen people acting from their Child ego state.

Everyone experiences the world in an individual way, being born as a unique person, having unique experiences and training. In childhood some people have unhappy or even brutal experiences they never forget; or they block them out of their awareness because of the pain of remembering. Others are not exposed to brutality but may receive very little affection or attention from the people around them. Still others experience mainly joyful, happy times. Most people have experienced some of each.

When you are acting now as you did when you were little, you are in your Child ego state. A little boy may act tough to get his father's approval, then later in life do the same thing to get what he wants. A little girl like Karen may feel that she can accomplish things only by being cute even when she's a grown woman.

Being in your Child does not mean that you are childish or foolish. It means you are feeling and acting like the little boy or girl you once were.

The Child ego state can be subdivided into three different parts: The Natural Child, The Little Professor, The Adapted Child. Even when people are grown, they use all three parts of the Child ego state. The three parts of the Child are diagramed as shown at left.

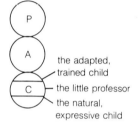

the adapted, trained child
the little professor
the natural, expressive child

the Natural Child

The Natural Child is the free, uncensored part. It is much like an infant—impulsive, curious, demanding, seeking and responding to touch. When you are doing whatever you want to do without thinking over the consequences, you are in your Natural Child. When you are feeling good, being inquisitive, acting self-centered, being playful or rebellious, you are also in your Natural Child.

the Little Professor

The Little Professor is the smart little kid in every person. Even without training, small children are creative, intuitive (they figure things out without much information), and learn to manipulate themselves and others to get what they want. When you know from the expression on a friend's face how he or she feels, you are using your intuitive Little Professor. When you create sand castles at the beach, or when you manipulate your face into a sad expression to make someone else feel sorry for you, you are using your Little Professor.

the Adapted Child

The Adapted Child is the trained or influenced part of the Child ego state. A bright little person who receives looks or glances that mean "Boy, you're dumb," and maybe hears words like, "You're sure a stupid kid," may adapt to feel stupid—not-OK. In other words, really smart children can adapt to think of themselves as stupid. If a person has learned to feel and act not-OK, to feel afraid, guilty, or ashamed, it is usually in this part of the personality. When you are older and still respond with these learned feelings about yourself, you are in your Adapted Child.

But the Adapted Child has also learned accepted manners, or common ways of speaking such as saying "thank you" or "please," which are necessary for people to live together harmoniously. For example, it would be unpleasant to sit at lunch beside someone in their Natural Child who burps, slurps, and spills food. In addition to the social graces, people need adaptations to protect their health and safety and to civilize them.

Many times people don't get along with each other or are suspicious of each other because their childhood adaptations are not the same. For example, there may be conflict at school if adaptations of a student differ from the expectations of a teacher. A teacher may expect courteous and respectful behavior. A particular student, however, may never have been taught to be courteous. The two of them will have a hard time getting along unless each of them in their Adult ego state finds out what's going wrong and why.

Sometimes adaptations work well for a *child* as defensive or protective devices. Sometimes they are self-defeating. For example, children with overly strict parents use three common forms of adaptation: withdrawal (tune out), compliance (submit), and procrastination (put it off). A child may discover that withdrawing from a tense situation at home is a protection against criticism, then later in life refuse to stand up for his or her rights when unjustly criticized in any situation. A child may get along well enough in his or her family or in school by complying with all expectations from authority figures. Later, that person may fail in a job or a friendship because of a lack and fear of independent thinking. A child may learn to get out of things by procrastinating—stalling when something is to be done—then fail to meet so many deadlines and obligations that she or he can't graduate with the class.

summary In summary, the Child ego state is an important part of the personality. Rage, violence, and destructiveness as well as affection and curiosity can come from the Child. It is the center of our most basic feelings about ourselves and others.

The ability to use and express the fun-loving, creative, intuitive, socially aware Child is important for good mental health. Finding out where destructive, violent, or helpless feelings come from, so that we can squelch the not-OK feelings of the Child ego state, is also important—important for the physical and emotional well being and for healthy, happy relationships with others.

exercises

1 evaluating case studies (group or individual)

Review the case studies at the beginning of the unit (page 37) and answer the following questions:

☐ Try to explain why Mike felt that his coach did not give him enough attention.

☐ How might Karen use the behavior she used with her father when she's older?

☐ Which part of her Child ego state was Karen using?

☐ What effects might Carlos' behavior have on his education? His vocation? His own family life?

☐ Which part of his Child ego state was Carlos experiencing in school?

☐ How would Sally's decision not to become an engineer affect her future?

2 Child ego state vocabulary and body language (group)

Ego states can be identified if you listen to the words a person uses and the tone of voice, observe body language, facial expressions, and postures. Tune into these nonverbal clues and make lists according to what you have observed as typical Child behavior.

Child words or phrases (e.g., wow, I wish)	*Child* gestures, postures, facial expressions, tone of voice
_____	_____
_____	_____
_____	_____

3 the Natural Child (individual or group)

Describe at least three situations in which the Natural Child might be expressed:

Negatively	*Positively*
at school _____	_____
_____	_____
at home _____	_____
_____	_____
with opposite sex ____	_____
_____	_____
with friends _____	_____
_____	_____

4 the Little Professor (individual or group)

Describe at least three ways the intuitive, creative, and manipulative Little Professor might be expressed:

Negatively	*Positively*
at school _____	_____
_____	_____
at home _____	_____
_____	_____
with opposite sex ____	_____
_____	_____
with friends _____	_____
_____	_____

5 the Adapted Child (individual or group)

Describe at least three ways the Adapted Child might be expressed:

Negatively	*Positively*
at school _____	_____
_____	_____
at home _____	_____
_____	_____
with opposite sex ____	_____
_____	_____
with friends _____	_____
_____	_____

suggested research

1 your inner Child

☐ Jot down three ways you now express your Natural Child.

☐ Jot down three ways you now use your Little Professor.

☐ Jot down three ways you now use your Adapted Child.

☐ Look at your list and decide whether or not your Child behavior is satisfying.

☐ If not, what might you want to change.

☐ What could you do so that your Child would be a happier part of your personality?

7 switching ego states

case study 1   Frank's grades are barely passing and he has several friends who are in a similar situation. Because of his sense of humor and ability to keep his classmates laughing, Frank is often called the class clown. At home, however, he acts very differently. As the only man in the household, he is serious most of the time. He helps with the housework, runs errands for his widowed mother, and participates in many of the decisions that are made about what to buy and where to go. Saturdays Frank has a job as an apprentice in a machine shop. He contributes part of this money for his board and room at home.

case study 2   Tom, a freshman, had been in an auto accident when he was young. He walked with a slight limp and was often ridiculed by two other students with, "There goes Tom, walking like a lame duck." Once, after orchestra rehearsal, where Tom played first violin, the other two ganged up on him, beat him with a chain, and broke his violin. During his hospital stay Tom became very depressed. Later his parents filed suit against the two students and Tom decided not to return to school.

case study 3   Jack and Brenda were juniors, worked hard at their studies, were on the honor roll, and were in love. Sometimes, when their parents thought they were at the library, Jack and Brenda were parked on an isolated road at the edge of town. Although Brenda said she shouldn't "go all the way," they frequently engaged in heavy petting. Eventually, she became pregnant.

case study 4   Jack hesitantly told a friend that Brenda was pregnant. First his friend joked, then he told him not to worry. Later he began to give Jack a lot of advice as to what to do and what not to do. At this point Jack got angry, told his friend he was all wrong and to keep his opinions to himself.

introduction to switching ego states   Have you ever been mad at yourself for some impulsive action? Or wished you thought, felt, or acted differently? Or been disappointed that you couldn't figure something out? Many people feel like this.

They act impulsively, changing ego states without knowing what they're doing and why. Sometimes this causes others to do or say what they later regret. With knowledge about ego states this problem can be helped. People can learn to recognize which ego state they are in and whether it is helpful or not in a given situation, so that they have more control over their responses. Switching ego states is useful and sometimes necessary. Being able to do so deliberately reinforces the feeling that one is OK—that one is a winner.

Perhaps you're a serious student and use a lot of Adult. Yet when you're on a picnic where the purpose is to have fun, you might want to switch from your Adult to your fun-loving Child. Or, when you need to think clearly, you may want to turn off your Child, who may feel hurt, depressed, rebellious, or excited and turn on your rational Adult. Or, when someone else needs to be taken care of, you can turn off your own Child and switch to a Nurturing Parent.

When your Adult is in control, you can decide which ego state to use. However, when the Adult is not in control, you may, for example, act bossy from your Critical Parent or have a temper tantrum from your Child ego state.

importance of each ego state

No one ego state is better than the others. Each ego state is valuable. For example, it's useful to have a Parent in your head that says, "Brush your teeth and wash your face". It's useful to have an Adult that knows how to read. It's useful to have a Child that enjoys a good laugh. People need all three aspects of their personalities in order to be complete.

People who are winners have all kinds of appropriate behavior available for their use. They can care about and nurture others. They can study and gather facts to be more productive and make reasonable decisions. They can express their fun-loving, joyful, curious, creative, sensuous Child and enjoy life.

However, sometimes a problem exists in an ego state which brings out that state's negative side. For example, there may be Parent advice or a Parent message that is destructive to the person carrying it around in his or her head. Or a person may have incomplete information and his or her Adult will not have enough data on which to make a decision. In addition, a person in his or her Child may have learned to feel inadequate or stupid. This holds a person back from developing fully and achieving desired goals. When there are problems in an ego state, a person can use the Adult to turn off the negative Parent and Child attitudes and behavior.

value clarification

Learning what each ego state values and needs can help a person clarify what he or she feels is important and why. This is an important step in the development of a winner.

When the values held by each ego state are in disagreement, a person will experience inner conflict. For example, a graduating senior boy might have a Parent ego state that values short hair for boys. The student's Child ego state may value the feel of long hair and the approval from his peers, or may value pleasing parents by keeping it short or rebelling against them by keeping it long. The student's Adult ego state may value getting a certain job. If his Adult is in control, he may estimate whether or not the length or style of his hair will affect his chances of getting it. When the values are similar about a particular issue, a person will not experience inner conflict in reference to it. For example, the Parent in a person may say, "Brush your teeth after eating;" the Child may say, "A clean mouth feels good and tastes good," and the Adult might say, "Clean teeth prevent cavities."

problems of switching ego states

To switch ego states whenever you want is an ability that can be developed with practice. Some people are able to be caring (like a good parent), rational (like an adult), and fun (like a healthy child) almost simultaneously. Or, they can easily switch from acting from their Parent ego states to their Adult or Child. At best, ego state boundaries are like permeable membranes, with psychic energy flowing through the boundaries from one ego state to another.

Some people have trouble switching ego states because they have a favorite ego state. They consistently use one or two and repress one or two. This is diagramed as shown at left.

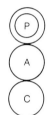

the Parent excluding the Adult and Child

Some people with rigid ego boundaries continually criticize others, advise others, or take care of others. They are defined as Constant Parents.

Some people continually analyze. They gather facts, evaluate the facts, make decisions, and act, most of the time, on the basis of facts, not of feelings. These people are defined as Constant Adults.

Some people act out their feelings most of the time. They may explode in anger, withdraw in guilt, argue defiantly, sulk resentfully, comply obediently. Or they may be constantly clowning, always "on stage." They may be helpless, dependent, and afraid to make their own decisions. Most seriously, they may destroy themselves with drinking or drugs or overeating. A person who continually responds on the basis of feelings is defined as a Constant Child.

the Adult excluding the Parent and Child

If you want to use some ego states less often and others more frequently, you can begin to change by figuring out first which ego state or states are the problem for you.

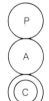

For example, if you have a bad temper or if you withdraw and sulk or if you burst out in tears easily or if you speak in a whispery voice that lacks authority, your Child has a problem. You will need to use your Adult to learn to stop and think and decide to do differently. This is not always easy. The more emotionally involved a person is, the harder it is to do. However, some simple techniques may be helpful.

the Child excluding the Parent and Adult

When you are about to explode from your Child or scold from your Parent, stop and count to ten. Take a few deep breaths. This will give you a little time to get your Adult tuned in. Or if you are afraid to speak up, decide to speak out at your next opportunity so that everyone can hear. Or if you are too bossy, begin to figure out how you can use more of your fun side.

exercises

1 evaluating case studies (group or individual)

Reread the case studies at the beginning of the unit (page 42) and answer the following questions:

☐ Which ego states does Frank seem to be in most often at school? At home? In the machine shop?

☐ Which ego states did Tom experience?

☐ Which ego states might his parents have been in? the boys who attacked him?

☐ How did Jack and Brenda switch ego states and in what situation?

☐ Which ego states were Jack and his friend in when Jack confided in him?

☐ Did either of them switch ego states? If so, why do you think they did?

2 switching ego states (group)

In small groups select a controversial subject for discussion such as whether or not schools need to offer a sex education program, or what should be done if someone comes to school high on drugs.

☐ Each person chooses one of the following ego state roles to play:

Angry Child   Thinking Adult   Critical Parent

Agreeable Child   Nurturing Parent

☐ Stay in the roles for 10-15 minutes while discussing the subject selected by the group.

☐ Then talk about how it felt when playing the parts.

3 egogram analysis (individual)

An egogram is one way to analyze how often a person uses each of his or her ego states. It illustrates which ego state is active what percentage of the time.[5]

☐ When making an egogram, decide on how long a period of time you wish to evaluate. An example of how one person's egogram might look during one hour at school is:

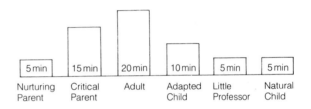

The above could be 5 minutes taking care of a friend, 15 minutes criticizing, 20 minutes studying, 10 minutes sulking, 5 minutes figuring out how to get a date, 5 minutes having a snack.

☐ Now make your own egogram. Think of what you did the past hour or yesterday, who you were with, what you felt, and how you acted.

☐ Draw your egogram for two typical situations.

☐ Is there any difference between the two? If so, why?

☐ Would you want to change anything? If so, how?

4 parent—teen switching ego states (group)

Here is the subject for a mini-play that needs a dialogue.

☐ Go into pairs and choose a role; one will be the student who gets home from a date at 4 a.m. The other will be the parent who is waiting for her/him.

☐ Each of you first writes your own lines. Make them real! A possible first parent line would be: I've been worried sick. Where have you been?

After you have written your dialogue, get into small groups of three pairs (six people) and have each pair act out their dialogue. Then discuss the following within the group:

☐ How it felt to be the parent.

☐ How it felt to be the student.

☐ How the parent acted differently than your real parents would have.

☐ Now discuss whether it was easier to argue or to keep peace.

suggested research

1 your ego state portrait

An ego state portrait is another way of discovering how often you use your Parent, Adult, and Child. It is drawn with three circles

of the size that represents your use of ego state. Common portraits are shown above.

☐ Draw three typical portraits of you.

    ☐ How you are at school.

    ☐ How you are at home.

    ☐ How you are with your friends.

☐ Do you like your portraits?

    ☐ If not, what do you want to change?

    ☐ How do you want to do it?

    ☐ When will you start?

☐ If you have time, draw ego state portraits of your parents, brothers and sisters, friends, or teachers.

8 putting the Adult in charge

case study 1   Gary lost his steady girl friend, his date for an important party. He became sulky and depressed; his stomach churned and several times he felt on the verge of tears—especially when he saw his ex-girlfriend walking and laughing with someone else. However, in front of his friends Gary acted as if nothing were wrong and he didn't care. After two weeks of feeling bad, Gary told himself, "It's time to snap out of it. I really liked her but if she's not interested in me, I know I can meet other girls." He made the decision to step up his social life and stop his sulking.

case study 2   Marie was overly solicitous with her friends and the children she baby-sat for. She fixed their lunch, poured their milk, and polished their shoes, much the same as her mother had done for her. The mother of the children she sat for asked her not to do so many things for the children but to help them learn how to do things for themselves. This request surprised Marie. She began to think about how often she acted parentally with three of her friends, and asked them if they liked it. All three said they liked it sometimes, when they felt sad, but didn't like it other times. Marie decided to be aware of and limit her oversolicitous behavior.

case study 3   Mr. Hernandez, the math teacher, had a heavy Spanish accent. Some students like him and tried to understand his different way of saying things. Some tuned him out and acted indifferently to his instructions and frequent offers to help. A few treated him with disdain by ridiculing him openly and behind his back. However, Mr. Hernandez did not seem to let the ridicule disturb him.

case study 4   Kathleen was terribly upset. She had just found out that her boyfriend had bragged and made up sex stories about her to impress his friends. She knew she had to go to her German class next period because of a big test the next day. Fighting back tears, she decided not to let these stories get her down. So she began counting in German as she trudged up the stairs. By the time she walked through the classroom door, she was calm and collected.

Adult functioning

Anybody can use the Adult ego state to change or control behavior. Have you ever tried to learn something new, found it difficult when first learning, but easier after practicing a while? Have you ever tried to do something, and not known how to go about it, then later figured it out? If so, you have been using and strengthening your Adult ego state. Like a muscle, the Adult grows stronger with use. The more it's used the more competent people are at using it.

For example, if a person has problems between the Parent and Child ego states, that person can learn to arbitrate and referee with the Adult (see diagram at left).

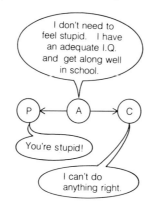

Or you might think of a diagram like this:

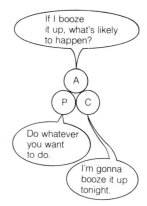

Or you might think of a diagram like this:

One of the reasons for strengthening the Adult is so that it can become the executive of the personality. Just like an executive in a business, the Adult takes charge of what is going on. The Adult-as-executive position doesn't mean that the person is always coming on from the Adult but that the Adult makes decisions about what is appropriate to use from the Parent or Child.

The Adult can take charge in many ways. In the Adult state a person can:

Referee when there is inner conflict between the Parent and Child

Act as a protector of the Child when it feels threatened

Set reasonable goals and determine procedures for achieving the goals

Select and use Parent behaviors appropriately

Select and use Child behaviors appropriately

Learn new ways of thinking and acting

For instance, if you are ignored by a friend while passing down the hallway, you can chose how to respond. You could feel mad, sad, depressed, or hurt. You could go to the friend and ask if anything is wrong. You could scold the person for being rude. People have more options on how to behave than they often realize. With their Adults as executives their choices might be improved.

48

foggy thinking

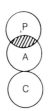

Parent contamination
of the Adult

Sometimes the clear thinking of the Adult is fogged up by Parent opinions and /or Child feelings. This is called *contamination*. Contamination means spoilage and that's what happens to the Adult. Its clear thinking is spoiled.

The spoiling may come from a Parent ego state learned from parent figures who were prejudiced against people of a different race, religion, sex, education, vocation, age, or life style. For example, if your father frequently expounded on "those crazy women drivers" you may be suspicious of all women when they are driving. You may think you are in your Adult when criticizing them, but actually your thinking is still being influenced by your father. Or as another example, if any of your parent figures said, "All men are beasts," you may also think of men as rude and cruel. You may believe this is an Adult fact when actually you are operating under the influence of a Parent prejudice.

The contamination can also come from a Child ego state if the person has learned to be unrealistic about himself or herself and about the world. For example, a little girl who learns to think of herself as dumb when she really isn't has a hard time thinking straight about her actual intelligence. A little boy who learns to think he's not a real boy because he's small and not good at football has a hard time accepting that he's an OK male.

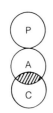

Child contamination
of the Adult

Some childhood illusions stick with people. No matter how old they are, most people believe in some form of magic. Some believe in the magic of *things*. They think things, such as new clothes or a new car, will bring them a new boy or girl friend. And sometimes it does. So the belief in magic is not surprising, after all.

Some people also believe that if they try hard enough, or wait long enough, something magical will happen. They keep on trying instead of doing; they keep on waiting instead of acting. They wait for a magical person who will come along and rescue them or at least make their lives more interesting.

Most peoples' Adults are contaminated by the Parent and Child ego states.

**decontaminating
the Adult**

Everyone's thinking is contaminated at times and the contamination is always related to specific stimuli. The process of decontaminating starts with Adult awareness of Parental opinions or Child feelings that have not been checked against reality. When a moment of awareness occurs, the ego state boundaries are realigned. The Child and Parent ego states do not overlap the Adult. So the Adult thinking is then clear about that particular subject.

Educating the Adult is the next step to clear thinking. This includes getting new information that may contradict the old Parent or Child tapes. It also includes practicing new behavior decided upon by the Adult.

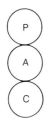

decontaminated Adult

One of the most effective ways to decontaminate is to examine the actual facts—to look at the facts that are already known and to determine what facts may still be needed before a decision is made. Many people make decisions primarily on the basis of their Child feelings or their Parent traditions. Both have value and the decontaminated Adult will consider these values without being bound by them.

exercises

1 evaluating case studies (group or individual)
Reread the case studies at the beginning of the unit (page 47) and answer the following questions:

☐ Which ego states did Gary experience initially?

☐ What did he seem to switch to?

☐ Which ego state was Marie using with both the children she baby-sat for and her friends?

☐ Was her change an effective one?

☐ What contamination influenced some students' attitudes against Mr. Hernandez?

☐ How could this affect their ability to learn from him?

☐ Which ego state did Kathleen experience at first?

☐ Which ego state had her boyfriend been in when he told the stories?

2 Parent contamination (group)

Work together in small groups very quickly (about ten minutes) without arguing a point (this is called brainstorming). Think of five or six commonly used adjectives for each of the subjects listed. Stick to those adjectives that we are likely to hear people use in everyday conversations.

Men are: Women are:

_____   _____

_____   _____

_____   _____

Teachers are: Parents are:

_____   _____

_____   _____

_____   _____

☐ Compare your personal opinion with those of the group. Discuss which common adjectives you, personally, agree with and which you, personally, disagree with and why.

☐ What other common contaminations do you see in your community?

3 sorting out opinions (group)

Discuss two of the following topics. Support your position to the others in your group by giving as many facts as you can. Debate the questions but attempt to come to a group consensus on both issues.

☐ Wars are a necessity and will always exist as they always have.

☐ Women were meant to perpetuate the race.

☐ Watching TV is like brainwashing.

☐ Students learn in proportion to how much they like the teacher.

☐ Men are less emotional than women.

After discussion, share your feelings with the group.

☐ What did you experience in the group when trying to reach a consensus?

☐ What did you do to convince the group of your view?

50

suggested research

1 Child contamination

Begin to become aware of how your Child ego state may affect your clear thinking by examining the following:

Do you often use words indicating that you are waiting for a magical person or event?

When (if only) he/she changes . . .

When (if only) I graduate . . .

When (if only) I get the right job . . .

☐ Do you often use words indicating that you think of yourself in one way and cannot change?

I can't help it that . . .

I'm so stupid that . . .

I'm so confused that . . .

☐ What do you frequently state about yourself?

I'm so . . . that . . .

☐ Now reverse any of the above assumptions you have made. For example:

He/she may never change so . . .

I'm so powerful that . . .

I'm so . . . that . . .

After you have considered possible Parent and Child contaminations, ask yourself the following questions:

☐ Am I satisfied with what I've discovered?

☐ What do I need to reevaluate?

☐ What do I need to change?

☐ What Adult questions do I need to raise?

2 strengthening the Adult

Look through a weekly news magazine or the daily newspaper for two or three articles about students. Read through the articles and decide which ego state the writer is speaking from and what ego state is being activated in you.

☐ Now go through the articles carefully and omit Parent and Child words.

Jot down your response to these questions:

☐ How does the use of certain Parent or Child words affect your Adult understanding of what the article is saying?

☐ How do these Parent or Child words make you feel?

☐ How does the article sound with the Parent and Child words omitted?

☐ What is our responsibility to ourselves and others in reporting such events?

9 taking care of the Child

case study 1 Tom's father, a doctor, was suddenly killed when his light plane crashed into a mountain. A sheriff came to notify the family and told Tom, "Now you've got to be the man." Tom, age 13, was the only man in the family. There were neither uncles nor close male friends to help him come to terms with his loss. Although Tom's mother grieved deeply, and frequently wept copious tears, Tom felt he could not do that, thought he must be strong, take care of her, and not show his own feelings.

case study 2 Mr. Ching, the U.S. history teacher, wanted to visit Peking where his parents had been born. He often talked about it in class and compared life in Peking, as his parents had described it, with the current situation, as described by the newspaper. One day a Board of Education member visited his class and at the end of the period reprimanded Mr. Ching for "not staying on the subject". Instead of getting angry or depressed, Mr. Ching explained the relevance of the subject in such a way that the visitor was satisfied. Mr. Ching felt very good about the way he handled the situation.

case study 3 Sharon started having headaches after she broke up with Troy. For a year, she and Troy had been dating until suddenly he began to act indifferent. When she passed him in the hall, he would start talking in a very animated way to whomever was near him. The Junior Prom was fast approaching, but Troy hadn't asked Sharon to go. In desperation Sharon called him one evening and told him she was making a new dress. Troy replied, "I hope it's not for the prom. My mom says we're together too much. Anyhow, I want to take someone else." After an hour of tears, Sharon called a boy who was new to the school and who accepted her invitation gladly.

caring for the Child Learning how to take care of the Child in oneself or in someone else is one of the most important uses of TA. Some people can do this easily, especially if they had affectionate, caring parents. Others really have to work at it, especially if they didn't get enough love, direction, and attention themselves. Most people have times when they feel down and need comforting. It's helpful at such times to have ways to take care of these needs.

You may not be in touch with this need in yourself so stop and think a moment. Have you ever been alone and unhaipy and wished someone were there to take care of you? Or have you ever needed help but felt unable to ask for it? Or have you ever wanted to make someone happy but felt anxious because you weren't sure of the response? In each of these situations, or similar ones, it is a Child ego state that needs to be taken care of. Sometimes what needs taking care of is your own inner Child; sometimes it is the inner Child of someone else. You can learn how to take better care of both.

People's Child ego state is often more active when they are hungry, sick, worried, tired, hurt, or afraid. Their Child then feels a need for something—food, sleep, comfort, encouragement, love, and so forth. If these basic needs are not met, the person feels worse. If they are met, one usually not only feels better but also is able to cope more adequately and to function more successfully.

caring with the Parent The Child ego state can be cared for in many ways. The first way is to use nurturing behavior from the Parent ego state. If you had nurturing parents you may copy them automatically. You will take care of your own inner Child and the Child in others as you were cared for in childhood. For example, if you have had a bad cold you are likely to go into your Child ego state and want orange juice if you got it and liked it when you were little. If you do give orange juice to yourself, you are using your Parent ego state to care for your own inner Child. At the same time you are also likely to think orange juice would be good for others if they have colds. In such cases you may again use your Parent ego state and take care of another person's Child, giving orange juice as a sign of caring.

Or another example: If you sometimes feel discouraged but had nurturing parents when you were younger and therefore a Nurturing Parent ego state, you can turn on those encouraging Parent "tapes" in your head and reassure yourself. Use phrases such as, "Don't worry, it will turn out all right in the end" or, "Just keep trying, you can do it." Or you may copy your parents and also say these things to others when they are discouraged.

caring with the Adult Another way of taking care of your Child is by using your Adult ego state which has been strengthened by reading books about children, observing good nurturing behavior, taking courses in child development, and thinking about what children need to be happy and healthy. When your Adult takes care of your own inner Child, you might, for example, look at yourself in the mirror and say, "Your skin isn't looking well. Perhaps too much chocolate. Let's go to the doctor and check it out."

When transacting in the Adult ego state with a friend who looks unhappy, a person might, for example, say, "You really seem unhappy today. Is there anything you'd like to talk about?" In other words, a person using the Adult ego state observes and processes data (i.e., face looks unhappy), then does probability estimating (i.e., talking might help).

If you wish to increase the playful, fun-loving Child part of your personality, your Adult will need to referee and decrease the Critical Parent part of your personality. One way to do this is to engage your Adult in an inner conversation with your Parent. The conversation might start with, "Hey, please relax a little. I'm just going to laugh and have some fun. I'm not going to hurt myself or anyone else."

Another way to increase the playful, fun-loving Child part of your personality is to complete those Adult chores or assignments that seem to be hanging over your head, making you feel uncomfortable. When you've completed things that are bugging you, you'll feel more like having fun.

childlike fun and fantasy   A third way to take care of your inner Child is to have childlike fun with the Child of someone else.

A common complaint people often make about themselves or others is that they "never have any fun" or "just don't know how to have fun" or "there's no one around to have fun with." To run with someone else along the beach, to play catch, to laugh at a joke are a few of the many ways the Child in you and in someone else will feel mutually accepted and cared for.

If there isn't anyone around to play with, you can have fun alone. The warmth of sun on your face, the coolness of water on your feet, a hike through the forest or fields may be ways of caring for your inner Child.

You may not be able to go to the forest and fields. If not, try fantasy. Is there something you know is OK to do but that you are afraid or embarrassed to try such as dancing, swimming, playing tennis? If so, use your imagination to get over this fear. See yourself in your fantasy doing the very thing you are afraid of. Be aware of how you are dressed, how you move, where you are, and so forth. Repeat this fantasy many times until you feel good about what you see. Then set aside a time to make the first step toward bringing your fantasy to reality.

Fantasy can also be used to give the Child a feeling of peace and quiet. Think of a time when you felt very comfortable and safe. Go back to that time and place in your imagination. Re-live the feeling once more. Your Child will feel cared for and that will feel good.

exercises

1 evaluating case studies (group or individual)

Reread the case studies at the beginning of the unit (page 52) and answer the following questions:

☐ Which ego states did Tom and his mother express most often according to the case study?

☐ Which feelings might Tom have had that he did not show? Do you think it was a wise choice for Tom to hide his feelings?

☐ How did Mr. Ching use his ego states?

☐ How did he take care of his inner Child?

☐ What options does Sharon have for taking care of her own inner Child?

2 childhood memories (group)

Each of the case studies in this unit showed Child ego state involvement. You probably feel comfortable enough by now to meet in groups of three for the following personal discussions. Take about five or ten minutes for each situation.

☐ Share with others the feelings you had when you expected something like an award or a present and didn't receive it. Include how you took care of yourself or how others did or did not take care of you.

☐ Share with others the feelings you had when you were ridiculed or criticized unfairly. Include how you took care of yourself and how others did or did not take care of you.

☐ Share with others the feelings you had when you came out victorious in a tough situation. Include how you took care of others and how others did or did not take care of you.

suggested research

1 a caring story

Write a short story that describes a child who needs to be cared for.

Write three different endings:

☐ With the child being mistreated

☐ With the child being ignored

☐ With the child receiving good care

2 caring for the forgotten

(This may need to be arranged through an institutional administrator or chaplain who will give you suggestions on what to say and do.)

Visit a convalescent home, or a state, county, or veterans hospital.

☐ Talk to two people there. Try to get a feeling for how they feel in their Child ego state.

☐ Take a small thoughtful gift with you or treat them to something from the canteen.

☐ Write up a brief summary of your experiences.

10 monitoring the Parent

case study 1 Terry never got into trouble but he often felt guilty inside and didn't know why. He lived with his father and his unmarried sixty-four-year old aunt because Terry's mother had died of complications from his birth. At least, that's what his aunt frequently told him. Whenever she was displeased in the slightest she would scowl, sigh, then shake her head with, "Oh, dear, some day you'll be the death of me yet, just like you were of your poor, sweet mother." Terry told his TA class that confronting his aunt would not change her so he didn't try. Instead Terry decided to work out his feelings on a punching bag in his garage whenever he felt guilty.

case study 2 Mrs. Polinski, the school principal, often got very angry at students if she caught them smoking. She shouted at them just as her father had in similar situations. One day a letter was placed on the principal's desk, signed by 40 students. It read, "Please stop yelling at us. We can hear you." Mrs. Polinski told her secretary that she was "about to have a stroke at the effrontery of the students." When her secretary said she agreed with the students, the principal sat down in a chair, took a deep breath and said, "You're right and I don't need to yell like my pa." At Christmas she received a beautiful desk plant and a big thank-you card signed by some of the students and her secretary.

case study 3 Cindy's mother was a nurse who tended to hover over people, pursing her lips while looking sympathetically at anyone who had even a slight cold. If someone was really ill, her mother would go into the full routine of nursing activity. Cindy did the same, totally unaware that it turned some people off, until one particular day. Her boy friend was in the hospital with a broken leg and Cindy, visiting him, was busily straightening out his bedside table and pillows. Suddenly he burst out with, "Hey, Cindy, you're not my nurse. Just sit down and talk to me, OK?"

Most people do not know when they are using their Parent ego state toward other people. They are also unaware when their Child is listening to the inner directions of their Parent. Like ventriloquists, they may treat others as dummies or act like dummies themselves.

Once people realize that they are responding automatically, they may see the need to monitor some of the Critical and Nurturing Parent behavior they use. A monitor is someone who checks up on things to see that whatever is going on is appropriate to the situation. The best monitor of feelings and behavior is the Adult ego state.

Anyone can learn to monitor the Parent ego state. That means one can learn when to use it and when not to use it, either with oneself or with others. It is a very useful technique. After all, even well-meaning parents hold opinions that are no longer relevant.

Obviously many things in the Parent ego state are valuable. Early parental messages such as, "Brush your teeth," "Watch out as you cross the street," "Be on time," are practical instructions that we needn't think about before following. However, even though they are useful instructions, a friend, or a younger brother or sister may not want to hear these commands from you.

Have you ever been told that you act exactly like your mother, your father, or like one of your other parent figures? Have you ever caught yourself voicing your parents' attitudes, opinions, or prejudices? speaking in the same tone of voice or using the same words they did? Most people do this from time to time, some more than others.

If you have become aware of this about yourself, are you pleased with the ways you copy them? If you don't think you copy them, perhaps it is because you are not aware of it, but other people may see it clearly. If you are often in your Child, you may also not be aware of how much you listen to your inner Parent.

Being aware and learning how and when to monitor your Parent may save you and others pain and resentment. This is particularly true if you have an over-protective or overcritical Parent ego state and use it a lot with others or with yourself.

Some *overcritical* parents say things such as, "You're stupid, you'll never amount to anything," or "I wish you'd go get lost." These negative messages are recorded in a child's brain. If something triggers them off, a person may use the Parent ego state and say similar things to someone else like "You're stupid!" or "Don't bother me."

In the Child ego state, the same person may hear these comments over and over and will feel stupid or rejected (as told to feel) and fearful of even existing. It's not unusual to hear a person say, in the middle of a discussion, "I don't get it. I must be stupid," or "I think I'll leave. Nobody ever listens to me."

Overprotective parents say things such as "Don't worry, I'll finish your job for you," or "You're too young to have to worry about such things." These kinds of messages are also recorded in the brain and replayed. In the Parent ego state they are used on others; in the Child ego state they give one a feeling of being unable to complete the work or think for oneself. Such people may become overly dependent, always looking for care and protection. They may say such things as "I wish somebody'd finish this job for me—I'm too tired. Or, "I don't want to think about it anymore."

Most parents have opinions about everything in general, and many things in particular, and these opinions sometimes need monitoring. For example, a Parent prejudice such as "Girls don't need a vocation, they'll just get married," when the facts say nine out of ten women will work, needs to be monitored and turned off. Or a Parent prejudice such as "If you don't play football, you're not a man," needs to be monitored and turned off; so do parental prejudices such as "Don't trust people who are different" or "Everyone should get married and have children."

inconsistent parents

Some parents are *inconsistent* and often say things such as "If you don't clean your room every day you'll get no dinner" and other times say things such as "Eat your dinner now and let your room go until the weekend". Another inconsistent parent might proclaim, "I worry about you and expect you *always* to be home at six o'clock" and the next week say something like "I don't care what you do, just leave me alone."

People who have inconsistent parents often are unsure of themselves. In their Parent ego state when baby-sitting for younger children, or when they are grown and have children of their own, they fluctuate in what they expect the children to do. They copy their own parents' inconsistent behavior. People like this may be called wishy-washy or unfair because they say one thing one day and something different the next.

Monitoring this kind of Parent ego state requires a decision to do things differently, to stick to what one says. Unless new facts provide a valid reason for changing a decision, consistency is a valuable parental attribute and can be developed by anyone.

conflicting parents

Some people have *conflicting* parents who argue a lot. The arguments may, for example, be loud, even abusive; or quiet, even rational; or bitter, even cruel; or laughable, even fun. Conflict may arise over work, education, money, leisure time, sex and sex roles, how to rear children, and so forth. Each parent may take an opposing view, such as: "Money should be spent" *vs.* "Money should be saved," or "Education isn't worth a damn" *vs.* "Education is the only thing worth fighting for," or "Women's place is in the home" *vs.* "Women should pay their own way."

People whose parents are in conflict with each other often experience an inner battle within their Parent ego state. The inner Child may listen, first to one parent and then to another. From the Parent ego state they may act toward others, first as one parent acted, then as the other parent acted. Such a person gets into arguments or goes looking for a fight as his or her parents did. When one knows the areas of conflict, the issues that one's parents argued or fought about, one will have new awareness and be able to monitor the inner Parent from time to time. Learning to monitor the Parent is a useful technique, not only to help one feel better about oneself, but also to relate better to others.

uninvolved parents

Some parents are *uninvolved;* they stay away from home a lot, or they don't listen, don't share their feelings and ideas. They isolate themselves in a particular room or workshop, or in front of the TV and say things such as, "Don't bother me, I'm busy." They act like the proverbial absent-minded professor, forgetting birthdays and other special occasions.

Such parents may stay uninvolved with people in general, tend to avoid them, keep people at a distance, and have relationships with others only on a superficial level. Other uninvolved parents may only act that way at home and get close to other people who are not part of their family.

People who have uninvolved parents often are cold and distant when in their Parent ego state. They will withdraw as their parents once did; when in the Child they will act friendly but unsure of themselves. They may search diligently for someone who will act like an involved parent but, at the same time, doubt that it could ever happen.

superorganized parents

Some people have *superorganized* parents who process data continually, who do not often show their Child ego state affection and impulsiveness, nor their Critical and Nurturing Parent. Such people overuse their Adult ego state. Whereas it is useful to have the Adult as executive, it is not useful to continually turn off the emotions and feelings in the personality.

People who have superorganized parents respond, from their Child ego state, with rebellion, indifference, or total compliance. However, when they are in their Parent ego state they will be very organized themselves and expect others to be likewise. Later, when they get a job, they may have unrealistic expectations of others.

overneedy parents

Some people have emotionally *overneedy* parents who continually expect to be babied and taken care of, or to be cheered up and reassured, or to be criticized and forgiven. Such parents often manipulate their children into taking parental roles at home. Role reversals between the actual parents and their children is not conducive to the development of winners.

People who have emotionally overneedy parents often choose to marry an overneedy person so that they have someone to take care of as they learned to do in childhood. Some people with this background have become so tired of caring for their parents and feel so inadequate at meeting their parents' excessive needs that they flip into the needy Child ego state themselves in a desperate effort to get attention.

Negative Parent patterns can be monitored toward more satisfactory behavior. People are often unaware of their Parent ego state behavior. Once the Adult ego state becomes aware, it can be used as a monitor. However don't monitor the good qualities of your Parent. Use them.

exercises

1 evaluating case studies (group or individual)

Reread the case studies at the beginning of the unit (page 56) and answer the following questions:

☐ How might Terry feel in his Child ego state when blamed for his mother's death?

☐ Why might Terry need to monitor his Parent ego state with himself and others?

☐ What would be some adjectives to describe Mrs. Polinski's Parent ego state?

☐ How and why did she learn to monitor it?

☐ Cindy was able to use her Nurturing Parent easily, but what might be various responses to it?

☐ What do you suppose Cindy was like when she was not acting like a nurse?

2 monitoring the Parent in role play (group)

Form groups of seven.

☐ Each group then selects a school problem to discuss.

☐ Each person in the group selects one of the roles to play during the discussion:

overcritical parent   overneedy parent

overprotective parent   overorganized parent

inconsistent parent   uninvolved parent

conflicting parent

☐ If there is enough time, do the exercise with one group in the center of the classroom for five to seven minutes and the others observing the process—like looking into a fishbowl. Then switch so a new group can get in the center and continue.

3 a winner of a parent (group)

Discuss and make a list of various parental characteristics that indicate winning qualities.

☐ How might people respond to this ideal parent?

☐ What decisions must a person make to become this kind of parent?

suggested research

1 monitoring specifics in the Parent

To know what negatives to monitor in your own Parent ego state make and complete a list like the following. Analyze each of the parent figures you had when you were little. Give examples of how each used behavior that, in you, needs monitoring.

	Parent 1	Parent 2	Parent 3
Overcritical	_____	_____	_____
	_____	_____	_____
Overprotective	_____	_____	_____
	_____	_____	_____
Inconsistent	_____	_____	_____
	_____	_____	_____
Conflicting	_____	_____	_____
	_____	_____	_____

Overneedy _____ _____ _____

_____ _____ _____

Overorganized_____ _____ _____

_____ _____ _____

Uninvolved _____ _____ _____

_____ _____ _____

Note: The above lists are only for the negative messages that need monitoring. Every parent sends positive messages. Don't monitor

those, use them when they are appropriate to a situation.

2 Parents in the news

Look through a few newspapers or news magazines. Select articles or pictures that give you a clue that someone might be in the Parent ego state and needing to monitor it.

☐ List some reactions different people might have to the Parent ego state as shown in the news article?

☐ Think about how the people described might monitor their Parent ego states and change their behavior.

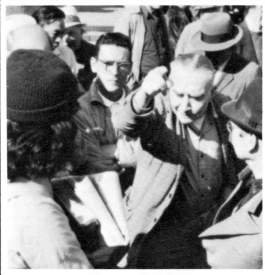

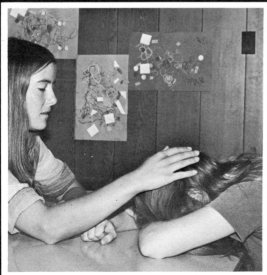

11 transactional theory

case study 1   Pete's mother was attractive, concerned, but was overindulgent and set no
standards for his behavior. He had never known his father and had become an
expert at conning women and antagonizing men. By the time he was thirteen, Pete
had already been on probation for three years for robbery and drug pushing. He
was eventually sent to a special school where he was consistently polite to the
women teachers but bad-mouthed the men.

case study 2   Zelma's mother died when she was ten years old. Her father was a truck driver who
worked long hours and often left her in charge of two younger sisters. Zelma worked
very hard trying to keep the house organized and felt very resentful when her sisters
were untidy or late for supper. She often complained that "nobody cared".

case study 3   Jose's parents were from Mexico and spoke only Spanish. Jose was bilingual,
speaking English at school and Spanish at home. One day at school, when he was
speaking Spanish to a friend, a new teacher took him by the shoulder and asked,
"Jose, are you planning some kind of trouble? Is that why you're not speaking
English?"

introduction to
transactions
Do you sometimes talk to someone and get a response that shows you are
understood? If so, the transaction is *complementary*. If you get a response that
leaves you feeling misunderstood or surprised, the transaction is *crossed*. Do you
sometimes say one thing but mean something else with your tone of voice or body
language. When you do, do you get a secret message back? If so, the transaction
is *ulterior*.

Learning how to say what you want to say and really be heard, and learning how
to hear what other people are really saying are signs of the winner in you.
Transactional Analysis proper is a way of analyzing this. It analyzes how the ego
states of one person interact with the ego states of another. The word "proper" is

used to distinguish this particular form of analysis from the total system of TA. When you say something to someone or look at someone in a certain way, you expect a specific response. This process of *sending* a message with words or facial expression is a *stimulus* called a stroke. If a person *responds* with words or facial expression, a stroke is being sent back and a transaction has occurred.

A simple transaction is diagramed by drawing two P - A - C diagrams side by side. One set of circles represents the person who initiates the transaction. The other set represents the person who responds. An arrow is then drawn from the active ego state in the first person to the ego state in the other that is to be "hooked". This is called the transactional stimulus. Another arrow is drawn similarly from the active ego state in the second person back to one of the ego states in the first. This is called the transactional response.

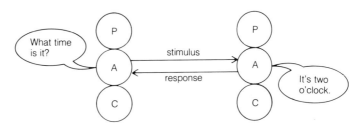

simple transactional diagram

A *stroke* is part of a transaction; it is any form of touch or recognition. Strokes are *positive, negative,* or *crooked.* A crooked stroke is one which on the surface seems positive but underneath carries a negative message. Two or more strokes make up a transaction.

The common greeting "Hello" and the response of "Hello" is called a two-stroke transaction. If the first person then adds, "How are you" and gets a response of "Fine," it is a four-stroke transaction. In this common, everyday greeting each person usually gives and receives two *positive* strokes in the interchange. Each will usually feel OK about the transaction because it is *complementary,* which means that the stimulus given gets the response that is expected.

In some situations, however, a person might smile and say "Hello" but, instead of getting an expected response, might get a frown and a grunt from the other person, or a put-off remark. Such an unexpected response is a stroke too, but a *negative* one. The initial stimulus is *crossed* by this response and the first speaker will feel discounted and misunderstood. (In diagraming a crossed transaction the lines are not always crossed but the meaning is.)

The third type of transaction to be analyzed is *ulterior* or crooked. Crooked transactions occur when someone sends a double stimulus by asking "When is the meeting?" while batting their eyes seductively or by someone asking "When is the

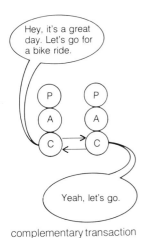

complementary transaction

meeting?" while looking downcast and sad. In both cases a nonverbal message is being sent. This is an *ulterior* stroke because it conceals a message different from the words that are used.

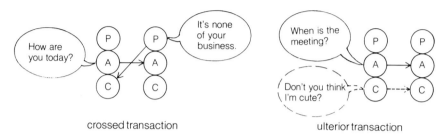

crossed transaction   ulterior transaction

Although complementary transactions are usually desirable because they keep communication flowing, it is useful to be able to identify crossed and ulterior transactions and cross the transaction in some situations.

For example, if you are critically accused, Parent to Child, of stealing something that you didn't take, a negative complementary transaction would be to become defensive and fight back or apologize from your Child. Crossing the transaction with "What data do you have?" might be more effective. Or an ulterior transaction, which could, for example, be given with a laugh of distain or look of disgust, might change the transactional pattern radically as in the following:

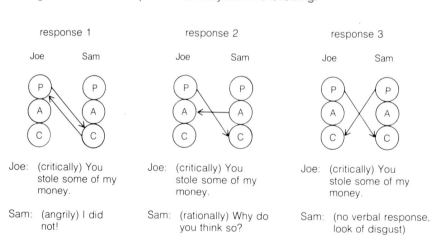

response 1

Joe   Sam

Joe: (critically) You stole some of my money.

Sam: (angrily) I did not!

response 2

Joe   Sam

Joe: (critically) You stole some of my money.

Sam: (rationally) Why do you think so?

response 3

Joe   Sam

Joe: (critically) You stole some of my money.

Sam: (no verbal response, look of disgust)

In the above situation the stimulus is sent from the Parent ego state to the Child. One way to respond is Child to Parent. The lines are parallel and communication is still open. Another way to respond is Adult to Adult with a crossed transaction. A third way is from critical Parent to Child. Each of these different responses will in turn, affect the next transaction.

exercises

1 evaluating case studies (group or individual)

Reread the case studies at the beginning of the unit (page 64) and answer the following questions:

☐ What kinds of transactions, with words and actions, might Pete have used with women or men—at home, at school, at work, in social situations?

☐ Which ego state do you think Zelma used most often when transacting with her sisters?

☐ How might their transactions be complementary, crossed, or ulterior?

☐ What positive, negative, or crooked strokes might Zelma have used with her sisters?

☐ How did the teacher appear to be transacting with Jose?

☐ What transactional options did Jose have?

☐ What positive, negative, or crooked strokes was the teacher giving Jose?

2 role-playing transactions (group)

Select a situation such as a high school student coming in after curfew and being met by an irate parent; or a student turning in a late paper.

☐ Briefly role play the situation.

☐ Those who are not in the role playing can identify the ego states and transactions.

3 diagraming transactions (individual)

Using the stimulus from the Adult, "What time is it?", think of some possible complementary, crossed, and ulterior verbal responses and diagram them.

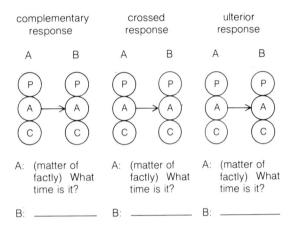

complementary response | crossed response | ulterior response

A: (matter of factly) What time is it?

B: _____

A: (matter of factly) What time is it?

B: _____

A: (matter of factly) What time is it?

B: _____

4 triad transactions (group)

(This exercise will take 25 to 30 minutes.)

☐ Divide class into groups of three.

☐ Each person will take a turn being speaker, listener, and analyzer in the small groups.

☐ The subject to be discussed is, "One of the biggest problems in our school."

☐ The roles of the triads are as follows:

—Speaker will talk about the subject as he or she perceives it.

—Listener will listen to what the speaker is saying and be actively involved in trying to understand. The listener will ask questions for clarification and draw the speaker out by giving feedback.

—Analyzer will observe and keep track of some of the complementary, crossed, and ulterior transactions and give feedback to the other two group members.

□ After seven to ten minutes the triads will switch. The speaker will become the analyzer, the listener will become the speaker, and the analyzer will become the listener. The same subject or a different one will then be discussed, following the same process.

—After seven to ten minutes switch roles once more so that each person in the triad has had a chance to play each of three parts.

suggested research

1 compatibility of ego states

Use these questions to analyze the relationship you have with a friend, parent, brother/sister; analyze the kind of transactions you usually have with this particular person.

□ Are all ego states—yours and the other persons—involved in your transactions?

□ Do you seem to operate from favorite ego states with each other most of the time?

□ If so, is this a good relationship? Does anything about it need to be changed?

2 transactions in drama

Look through the dialogue in a play. Select two examples of complementary transactions, crossed transactions, and ulterior transactions.

□ Which ego states seem to be involved in each example?

□ Are these transactions positive or negative in effect?

□ Why do you think this?

12 complementary transactions

case study 1   Sherry and Deanna lived in a group home supervised by competent "house parents". Although the parents were good cooks, the two girls often went on a cooking spree together, making goodies for the younger kids who also lived there and for their classmates at City High. However, both Sherry and Deanna would become very irritated and critical if anyone snitched their chocolate chip cookies without their permission. If they caught someone in the act, they usually forced an apology from the culprit.

case study 2   Christopher and Michael were identical twins. In school their teachers were usually frustrated because they were unable to tell them apart. If one became sick, the other would also. If one performed well or poorly, the other would do likewise. Christopher and Michael liked being twins (after all, that relationship was what they knew best) and frequently played tricks on their teachers and friends by pretending to be the other twin.

case study 3   The social studies class was working in small groups. Each group was instructed to plan a project and accomplish it within three weeks. Group 1 had a number of heated discussions before deciding on their project. Phrases such as "You're stupid" and "Nobody pays any attention to what I say" and "What makes you think you know it all?" were often overheard. Group 2 acted indifferent. During the planning period the words, "I don't know" or "Who cares?" were often heard. Group 3 members each wrote down what they wanted to do and then discussed which project was most practical. The words "I think" and "What do you think?" were often overheard.

case study 4   Heather, a sturdily built six-year-old, loved her ballerina doll. With a key on its back the doll could be wound up to twirl around on one foot. For months Heather tried to do the same but was unsuccessful. One day a new family moved next door and to

Heather's delight the family included a high school senior who was preparing to be a professional ballet dancer. Soon she was teaching her young neighbor who learned so quickly that before the year was out Heather had a solo dance in a large Christmas pageant.

introduction to complementary transactions

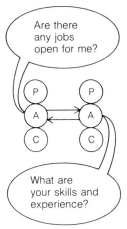

Hey, the boss is out of town today.

Whee, now we won't have to look so busy.

salesperson to salesperson - joking

Are there any jobs open for me?

What are your skills and experience?

applicant to interviewer - asking and receiving information

A complementary transaction occurs when the stimulus given by one person gets the response that he or she expects from another person. A complementary transaction is not the same as a compliment, although it may be one. A complementary transaction is when the lines between the ego states are open, usually parallel. When this is the case, communication can continue indefinitely between the people involved. Anytime you express yourself from any of your ego states and get the response you expect, you are likely to be involved in complementary transactions.

There are several kinds of complementary transactions. All are easy to recognize. For example, if you're feeling playful and tell someone a joke and that person laughs and jokes back, you are having a complementary Child to Child transaction. If you ask someone for information and they give it to you, you are having a complementary Adult to Adult transaction. If you and a friend talk sympathetically about neighbors who, for example, got flooded out of their homes, you are having a complementary Parent to Parent transaction. If you observe a crying child and do something helpful, you are having a complementary Parent to Child transaction.

Complementary transactions can be related to the job, as shown at left.

When people decide they want to go to work, all three of their ego states may be involved before they apply for a job. The Adult may read the want ads or go to a placement agency; the Parent may send inner messages to the Child such as "You can do anything you want to do, just keep trying," or "You could sell refrigerators to Eskimos with your gift or gab" or "You'll never get a job, you're so lazy" or "You can't trust people, so watch out what you say". The Child will hear these messages and will feel encouraged to go job hunting or will feel fearful and inadequate and unable to even approach the potential employer.

When the day or hour actually arrives and a job interview is scheduled, this same person's ego states may each get into the act and initiate and respond to transactions that turn out to be complementary or the person may be so anxious in the Child or critical in the Parent that the transactions are crossed, communication breaks down, and the job is lost.

It's not unusual to fill out an application, take it in fearfully to a prospective employer, and be met with a frown. The frown may be in response to the application, or may be the outward manifestation of a headache, or may be due to some family or other concern which is not related to the hiring of new personnel. Nevertheless, the Child ego state of the applicant is likely to observe the frown and may jump to erroneous conclusions. The Adult ego state needs to be the executive of the personality when applying for a job. Thus, transactions are likely to be complementary and successful.

friendships and ego states

Relationships such as friendships, teacher-student, parent-student, and husband-wife which are happy and long-lasting often have an abundance of complementary transactions.

Relationships with a variety of transactions are often the most rewarding. If two people are able to take care of each other when either is down, if they solve problems together by thinking things through, if they laugh and play together, they are using the full spectrum of their possible ego states. Sometimes they transact from the Nurturing Parent, being sympathetic and caring. Sometimes they transact from their Adults, gathering and using information to solve problems. Sometimes they transact from their playful, fun-loving Child ego states. Such an ability to switch ego states in appropriate ways to meet the needs of the moment makes for a satisfying relationship.

However, sometimes people get locked into a relationship that mainly draws on behavior from one ego state in each person. When this happens, the people seem stuck. It commonly occurs when one person comes on as a Parent most of the time and the other comes on as a Child in return. This makes for a very limited relationship.

complementary transactions in marriage or other close relationships

The main value of complementary transactions is that communication remains open, but a relationship that works only on one or two ego state levels is likely to be static instead of dynamic.

In a marriage, for example, many people unknowingly choose a substitute parent—someone who will take care of them, either the way they were taken care of when they were little, or the way they wish they had been cared for when they were little.

In any successful relationship it is appropriate to use caring parental behavior towards each other from time to time, but if someone wants it constantly or gives it constantly, the relationship is likely to become a losing one. Usually a relationship *primarily* based on Parent-Child complementary transactions becomes boring or frustrating to one or both persons involved. This might also happen if the relationship is primarily Adult to Adult and the people involved seldom have feelings toward one another.

exercises

1 evaluating case studies (group or individual)

Reread the case studies at the beginning of the unit (page 69) and discuss the following questions:

☐ What were the complementary transactions between Sherry and Deanna when they were cooking? Diagram them.

☐ What were the complementary transactions when they were giving goodies to others? Diagram them.

☐ Was there any switch in their ego states? If so, diagram it.

☐ What kinds of complementary transactions might teachers use when talking together about Christopher and Michael?

☐ What kind of complementary transactions would Christopher and Michael use between themselves when playing jokes on others?

☐ Diagram the various complementary transactions that might have gone on in each social studies group.

☐ Guess at how Heather might have felt about herself and her dancing before her new neighbor friend moved in.

☐ Discuss the kinds of transactions that Heather and her new friend were likely to have had and what this may have meant to Heather's self-image.

2 designing complementary transactions (group)

In your group design a complementary response to the sentence, "Have you seen my homework assignment?"

☐ First design it as a straightforward question and show two possible complementary responses:

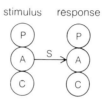 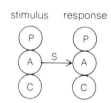

S: Have you seen my   S: Have you seen my
   homework assignment?   homework assignment?

R: R:

☐ Now diagram it as a whining question, "Gee, have you seen my homework assignment?" Show two possible complementary responses:

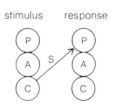 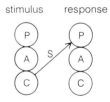

S: Gee, have you seen my   S: Gee, have you seen my
   homework assignment?   homework assignment?

R: R:

☐ Now as a bossy statement, "I want you to help me find my homework assignment right now!" Show two possible complementary responses:

□ Discuss how they can be arranged most effectively, then paste them on poster board or large sheets of paper.

□ After you've finished, discuss the complementary transactions that occurred in your group as you were working together.

suggested research

1 complementary dialogues

□ Write one paragraph of dialogue using only Child to Child transactions.

□ Write one paragraph of dialogue using only Parent to Parent transactions.

□ Write one paragraph of dialogue using only Parent to Child transactions.

□ Write one paragraph of dialogue using only Adult to Adult transactions.

2 positive transactions

Think back on the transactions you've had this past two weeks. Which ones particularly made you feel good? Now diagram the transactions.

□ Which ego states were involved?

□ Why did it feel good?

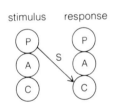

S: I want you to find my homework assignment right now!

R:

S: I want you to find my homework assignment right now!

R:

3 complementary transaction collage (group)

Go through magazines and select those pictures that illustrate complementary transactions.

13 crossed transactions

case study 1 Students were often discussed in the teachers' lunchroom and Morty's name frequently came up in the conversation. He was, according to several of his teachers, someone who could be "counted on to get himself into trouble." When assignments were given out, Morty would act as though he hadn't heard. When the teacher would ask for quiet he might explode with a silly laugh or drop his books or do something else that would disturb the class.

case study 2 Mrs. Anderson was feeling very uncomfortable. She didn't want to go to the school's open house because she was afraid that her twins Christopher and Michael would be criticized and she just couldn't take it. Mr. Anderson didn't want to go because he had "never liked school." Both of them had had unpleasant experiences with teachers when they were young; now whenever they visited their children's school they felt defensive but felt obligated to go. When one of the teachers told them that she was amused by one twin's trick of pretending to be the other twin, they looked confused and seemed unable to talk.

case study 3 Joanna felt very depressed. Her father had lost his job because of a company cutback in construction and he had started to drink heavily. For weeks the family tried to avoid him because he sometimes became brutal. At night Joanna would toss and turn for hours, often unable to sleep, often having frightening nightmares. At school she fell behind in her work and sometimes went to sleep in class. She did not talk to anyone about it until one day in desperation, she exploded to Alice, a classmate, about what was happening at home. Alice started complaining about her own situation instead of sympathizing.

introduction to A crossed transaction occurs when the ego state from which a person responds is
crossed transactions not the ego state response that was expected by the person who sent the stimulus. The lines between the ego states cross and communication usually breaks down. If you sometimes feel misunderstood, then it's likely you were involved in a crossed transaction.

For example, if you ask someone for the time and the response is, "Why don't you wear a watch of your own?", it's a crossed transaction. You asked for information, Adult to Adult, and instead got a crossed transaction, Parent to Child, as diagramed below left.

Or if you get a whiny response, "Gee, why are you always asking me?", it's also a crossed transaction, this time from the other person's Child to your Parent, as at right.

stimulus   response

S: What time is it?
R: Why don't you wear
    a watch of your own?

stimulus   response

S: What time is it?
R: Gee, why are you
    always asking me?

Crossed transactions do not always start with an Adult stimulus. For example, a Parent criticism designed for the Child might instead get another Parent criticism back, as diagramed below left.

Another crossed transaction occurs if a genuine plea for help from a Child ego state is met with a refusal or a put-down from another person (righthand diagram).

stimulus   response

S: You clumsy fool!
    Why don't you look
    where you're going?
R: You're the stupid one.
    Get your big feet out
    of my way.

stimulus   response

S: I never understand my
   homework. Will you
   help me?
R: Help *you*? I've got
   problems of my own!

crossing transactions   Sometimes it is useful to be able to cross a transaction deliberately. It's a way of changing the subject or stopping a psychological game. For example, if someone is rambling on and on, crossing the transaction may be more useful than saving up feelings of resentment. However, the person who is crossed may in turn feel resentment.

Crossed transactions often have an element of surprise.

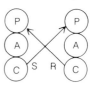

S: Stuff like this keeps
   happening to me all
   the time.
R: It might help to figure
   out why.

S: I've got troubles.
R: How about listening to
   mine for a change?

**crossed transactions
in close relationships**
When two friends stand glaring at each other, turn their backs on each other, are unwilling to continue transacting, or are puzzled by what has just occurred between them, it is likely that they have just experienced a *crossed transaction.* At this point, they will tend to withdraw, turn away from each other, switch the conversation in another direction, or start an argument. Much of the pain in everyday transactions with friends comes from crossed transactions.

The problem of too many crossed transactions in close relationships such as friendship or marriage is that somebody usually feels puzzled, put down, or misunderstood. This leads to further cross-ups and more resentments as shown in the following two examples:

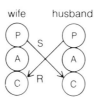

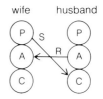

Wife:
I'm sick and tired of
picking up your clothes.
Husband:
Well, I'm sick and tired of
going to work every day.
Picking up clothes is your
job.

Wife:
I'm sick and tired of
picking up your clothes.

Husband:
Don't do it, then.

This kind of argument could go on and on, or it could be switched by using a complementary transactional response such as:

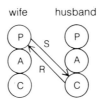

wife   husband

Wife (critically):
I'm sick and tired of
picking up your clothes.

Husband (apologetically):
I'm really sorry for leaving
you a mess to clean up. .

These kinds of parallel complementary transactions can be continued indefinitely:

(P-C) Wife:	"I'm sick and tired of picking your clothes up and feel like hitting you."
(C-P) Husband:	"I'm sorry for being so messy."
(P-C) Wife:	"You're always sorry, but what are you going to do about it?"
(C-P) Husband:	"I really don't know."
(P-C) Wife:	"Oh, I'm so mad at you."
(C-P) Husband:	"Please don't be mad at me."
(P-C) Wife:	"Well, you never do what you promise."
(C-P) Husband:	"I guess you're right. But I will this time."

A pattern of complementary transactions can be quickly changed if a cross is given:

(P-C) Wife:	"I'm sick and tired of picking your clothes up and feel like hitting you."
(A-A) Husband	(suddenly crosses): "What do you think that would accomplish? How about you taking care of your things and I'll take care of mine."

Furthermore, the same initial stimulus can be crossed with Parent-Child response:

(P-C) Husband: "Stop nagging—I'm tired of listening to you."

If a marriage relationship is stuck in a Parent-Child complementary transaction and one person decides to change, cross transactions will occur. This could result in a growing, more dynamic relationship or it might result in the couple deciding to split up. Crossing a transaction may be the start of changing a stereotyped relationship. However, some people prefer to keep things as they are.

uncrossing crossed transactions

Crossed transactions can be avoided in the first place or can be uncrossed when they are recognized.

If you wish to avoid a crossed transaction, you can do so by "playing your hunch." This is guessing from which ego state the stimulus was sent and which ego state it was intended to hit and responding with a complementary transaction.

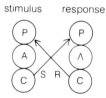

S: Boy, I feel terrible.
R: (crossed): How do you
   think I feel!

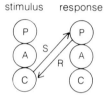

S: Boy, I feel terrible.
R: (complementary) "Yeh, you
    look as if you feel a little rocky.

summary

Crossed transactions can be useful, even necessary, at times, but communication is usually interrupted when they are used.

exercises

1 evaluating case studies (group or individual)

Reread the case studies at the beginning of the unit (page 74) and discuss the following questions:

☐ Which ego states did Morty frequently use to cross up his teachers?

☐ What kind of transactions might Mr. and Mrs. Anderson use at home when talking about their own school experiences?

☐ What kind of transactions might they have and with whom when attending the open house?

☐ What kind of response did Joanna expect from Alice?

☐ What kind of response did she get? If complementary, from which ego state to which ego state? If crossed, from which ego state to which ego state?

2 designing crossed transactions (group or individual)

Design two crossed transactional responses to each stimulus:

S: Do you know where
   the dictionary is?
R:

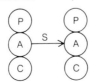

S: Do you know where
   the dictionary is?
R:

S: I'd like to leave by
   3 p.m.
R:

stimulus   response

S: I'd like to leave by
   3 p.m.
R:

S: I have a terrible
   headache.
   It just won't quit!
R:

stimulus   response

S: I have a terrible
   headache.
   It just won't quit!
R:

S: Don't you think you
   should get to bed
   earlier?
R:

S: Don't you think you
   should get to bed
   earlier?
R:

Choose the most common and the most unusual transactions from your group to share with the class.

3 crossing and uncrossing a transaction (group)

Pair up with someone you do *not* know well or would like to know better. One is the speaker, the other the listener.

☐ Speaker tells listener three things he/she likes about him/herself.

☐ Listener will first agree (creating a complementary transaction), then will disagree (creating a crossed transaction).

☐ Now switch roles and do the same thing.

☐ Discuss whether it was easy or hard to say something nice about yourself and if so, why.

☐ Switch roles again.

☐ Speaker tells listener three things he/she likes about the other.

☐ Listener will first agree (creating a complementary transaction), then will disagree (creating a crossed transaction).

☐ Now switch roles and do the same thing.

☐ Discuss what was comfortable and what was uncomfortable about the exercise.

suggested research

1 diagraming case studies

☐ Reread the cases at the beginning of this unit (page 74).

☐ Draw and label four sets of diagrams to illustrate the transactions.

2 crossed transactions on TV

As you watch your favorite TV situation drama see if you can recognize at least three crossed transactions.

☐ How would people feel at the end of the crossed transaction?

☐ Are these transactions positive or negative for the people involved?

☐ When might a crossed transaction be a useful thing to use?

3 getting in touch with your transactions

Think back over the past two weeks:

☐ Jot down at least four crossed transactions that you experienced.

☐ Were these positive or negative experiences?

☐ What could you have done to have made each of these transactions go more smoothly?

14 ulterior transactions

case study 1 Keith was a quiet, polite boy who never talked back although he often made obscene gestures when people turned away from him. Both his teachers and parents said he was no trouble. When the police called on Keith's parents and said he'd been caught red-handed stealing firearms, they found it hard to believe. His mother, wringing her hands, repeated over and over, "But he's always been such a good boy and I've never seen him angry."

case study 2 Ms. Johnson, the chemistry teacher, was known for her short temper. If someone disagreed with her in the slightest way, Ms. Johnson would become very irritated. She would walk heavily back and forth in an agitated manner, taking long steps, putting her heels down sharply. She often scowled disapprovingly while asking students, "Would anybody like some help?" Students in her classes learned that the way Ms. Johnson walked and looked at them was the key to her real mood.

case study 3 Mr. Kaplan, the Dean of Boys, was well liked. He had an appointment book hanging on his door and students who wanted to talk to him could do so by writing their names opposite the available time. When talking to people, Mr. Kaplan seldom sat behind his desk. Instead, he sat in one of two comfortable chairs, invited his visitor to sit down too, closed the door, and, if the discussion seemed important to the student, he did not even answer the phone.

case study 4 Margie often looked downcast when she asked her teachers for information. If they asked, "What's the matter?" she would just shake her head and walk away. Margie seldom finished her work and if a teacher became frustrated with her, she would complain, "Nobody ever has time to help me."

introduction to ulterior transactions Ulterior transactions are more complex than complementary and crossed ones. They differ in that they always involve more than two ego states at the same time. When an ulterior message is sent, it is disguised under a socially acceptable level.

Such is the purpose of the old cliche: "Come up and see me sometime!" On the surface (*overtly*) this is a social invitation from Adult to Adult; underneath (*covertly*) it often is a message from Child to Child, implying a sexual invitation.

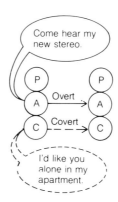

Sometimes the underlying message is hinted at fairly obviously, sometimes it is so well hidden that one is not consciously aware of it—as in many psychological games.

The ulterior or hidden part of the message can also be sent nonverbally by facial expression, body posture, tone of voice, and gestures. Looking downcast, flirtatious, angry, or disappointed rather than saying outright how one feels are but a few of the ways an ulterior stimulus or response can be given.

For example, if a boy asks a girl for the time and she looks up flirtatiously, tilts her head, and answers, "Wouldn't you like to know?", she is not answering the overt question but posing an ulterior teasing question of her own to hook his Child. He may grin and tease back or get angry and turn her off.

Body posture conveys ulterior messages in many ways. It is a language of its own. If a person sits with shoulders pulled in, hands clasped tightly, and head bent down, the message given will be quite different from that of a person standing with feet apart, hands on hips and chin jutting forward. Still another message is sent if a person sits casually and relaxed while relating bad news. Sometimes body language conveys a hidden meaning. For example, if a student who's been in trouble with the law is placed on probation and laughingly tells someone about the incident, the person is sending two messages (the ulterior is shown with a dotted line, as at left).

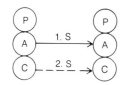

1. S. I've just been put on probation.
2. S: (I'm a loser. Ha! Ha!)

Clothes also convey a message. They may indicate that the wearer feels sexy, happy, depressed, independent, conforming, timid. They may reveal or hide the wearer's financial status, and show whether one cares about oneself or not. In addition to clothes, grooming also sends a message about how people feel about themselves and others. Grooming often reveals winner or loser self-concepts.

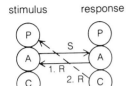

stimulus   response

S: Are you coming?
1. R (overt):
Yes, I'm coming.
2. R (covert):
(Quit bugging me.)

The tone of voice a person uses is another clue to the real message. "Yes, I'm coming," may be said with affection and warmth. It may also be shouted impatiently to convey resentment for being disturbed, as shown at left.

Ulterior transactions often are sent verbally as well as nonverbally. Perhaps you've seen a salesperson who says to a customer, "That makes you look very sophisticated!" when the style may not look good on that person.

A student who complains to his mother, "John's folks bought him a class sweater!" may say in effect, "You are not as good a mother as John's." The same kind of hidden meaning is suggested when Sally objects that "Mary's mother lets her stay out after midnight!"

If a teacher looks over a report saying, "I guess I didn't give you enough time on this," a message could be sent to two ego states in the student:

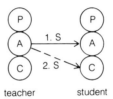

teacher   student

1. S (overt):   2. S (covert):
I guess I didn't give you   (This is not good enough.
enough time on this.   *You* didn't take enough time.)

The student, in turn, may hear the words from any ego state. If Adult, the response may be:

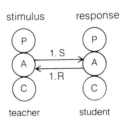

stimulus   response

teacher   student

1. R: That's right. It's at
least a three weeks project
and I only had ten days.

-or-

1. R: No, I had enough time.
I just didn't start it early enough.

83

The Child response may be:

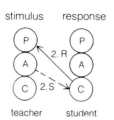

stimulus   response

teacher   student

2. R: Gosh, I did it wrong again.

-or-

2. R: That teacher always makes mistakes and blames it on me.

gallows transactions   Another important ulterior transaction is colloquially called the "gallows transaction."[6] This occurs when one makes jokes and laughs about one's self-destructive behavior. In essence, the laugh says, "Don't take me and what I say seriously." It also invites the listener to laugh in response, thus confirming that the person making the joke is in fact not to be treated seriously. For example, a young man might laughingly tell his friends, "I smashed up my car again last night." In other words, while he is telling about self-defeating behavior, he smiles as if it is clever. He thus reinforces the Child to keep himself in trouble. The laughing response from his friends also reinforces his self-defeating behavior.

The real issue that needs to be talked about is thus avoided. Nobody says, "Why are you laughing? It's not funny." Such a serious response might at first feel uncomfortable, but it would effectively take off the noose by refusing to go along with this self-destructive pattern.

The most common way to diagram a gallows transaction is:

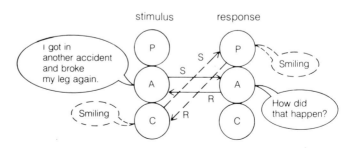

stimulus   response

sweatshirts and ulterior transactions

One of the colloquial words used in TA is *sweatshirt*. It means that people in the Child ego state unknowingly wear a message—much like a message printed on a sweatshirt.

Sweatshirt messages are usually part of an ulterior transaction—positive or negative—and are characteristic of the person.

The person wearing the "sweatshirt" wants other people to get a particular message such as "I'm tough, keep your distance;" "I'm helpless, take care of me;" "I'm smart, admire me;" "I'm nice, approve of me;" "I'm stupid, criticize me;""I'm sexy, come and get me;" and so forth. The message sent is often very obvious to others, sometimes it is more subtle.

Sweatshirts often determine the kinds of transactions people have. One person may convey a "kick me" message by being stoop-shouldered and looking anxious and consequently may get what he's looking for. Another person may send an "I'm tough" message by swaggering and jutting out a lower jaw and getting other people to be afraid or getting them to fight back.

Some people wear more than one message, one on the front and one on the back, or underneath. The front or public message is more obvious. It is what they hope other people will think about them. The less obvious message may only be seen in a close relationship. For example, a person may publicly come on with a "Look how clever I am," but at a deeper, private level wear a shirt marked "Don't get too close. I'm afraid I'm dumb," Another person's obvious message might be, "I'll help you get out of trouble," but at a deeper less obvious level may convey the threat, "If I do help, you'll pay for it."

Some people seem to wear one kind of sweatshirt in school or at work, another at home, and a third one with their friends at a party. Their message may vary from positive to negative, from obvious to quite hidden.

If you know how you want people to respond to you, you can probably guess what your public sweatshirt says. If you analyze how you feel about the responses you get, you may decipher your private sweatshirt message. You may want others to think you're tough or sweet, obedient or rebellious. You may want others to think you can fix everything up, straighten everything out, and solve everybody's problems, and secretly blame them for taking advantage of you. Or you may want others to think you're helpless, unable to think for yourself or take care of yourself, and secretly resent their treating you that way.

People treat you according to the "vibes" you give off. When you become aware of your winner and loser vibes, you gain more information to change what you want to change.

ulterior transactions in friendship

People are atracted to each other for many reasons. Common interests such as stamp collecting, drama club activities, or sports may bring people together on one obvious level of their personality. However, on a more hidden level it might be the sweatshirt that is the big attraction.

Personal feelings of worth or worthlessness are often the "glue" that keeps people together. People who feel weak and act that way often attract people who act superior. Without knowing it, the apparently stronger covers a weakness by taking care of and "lording it over" the apparently weaker.

In a positive friendship where honest caring exists, people are sensitive to the nonverbal messages from the other as well as being aware of their own motives. Instead of implying "You're too dumb, I'll do it," a real friend will say, "Try it. I think you can do it." Instead of saying, "You haven't any guts," the response might be, "I'm afraid too, but it's still worth trying."

ulterior transactions in marriage

Many ulterior transactions in marriage result from the sweatshirts worn during courtship. During the courtship each sends a not-so-hidden message that hooks the other. For example, the "I'm-helpless-please-take-care-of-me" shirt, attracts the "I'll-take-care-of-you" shirt. The "Look-how-smart-I-am" shirt may hook a complementary shirt that reads, "I'm stupid, tell me what to do." The sweatshirt reading, "I'm mean, I'll put you down," may attract the "I'm-guilty-punish-me" shirt.

After marriage, ulterior transactions generally continue. She may hint (i.e., with downcast eyes or a pout) to be taken out to dinner. If he gets the hint, he may make a positive or a negative response.

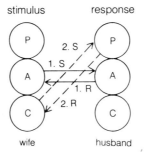

1. S: What are we going to do tonight?
2. S: (A pout that sends a message, "Poor me. Nobody loves me.")

1. R: Shall we go out to dinner?
2. R: (A frown that sends a message, "You know we can't afford it, but we'll do it anyway.")

Marriages that rely on an abundance of ulterior transactions are likely to be unhappy ones. The people involved may never be honest and open with one another. Rather than directly asking each other to meet their needs and then talking it over, they use devious manipulation to get what they want.

exercises

1 evaluating case studies (group or individual)

Reread the case studies at the beginning of the unit (page 81) and answer the following questions:

☐ What kinds of ulterior transactions did Keith probably use with his mother and teachers?

☐ What were the ulterior messages Ms. Johnson gave her students and how did she give the messages?

☐ What are various responses the students might have made to Ms. Johnson's messages?

☐ What kind of positive messages did Mr. Kaplan give and how did he give them?

☐ What messages did Margie give and how did she give them?

2 designing ulterior transactions (group or individual)

Design the dialogue for ulterior transactions that would fit the following diagrams: (1) decide what is actually said, and (2) determine the hidden meaning.

Be prepared to share with the entire class one of your ulterior transaction examples.

3 common sweatshirts (group)

Discuss the kinds of sweatshirt messages you see commonly around school. Develop a list of four or five.

☐ What kinds of postures, gestures, and voice tones would a person have to use to convey these messages.

☐ Now select one of these messages and develop a role play for someone in your group to present to the entire class. Have the class guess what the sweatshirt is that's being acted out.

4 group ulterior transaction (group)

Discuss any ulterior transaction that occurred between members of your group while you were working on the other exercises.

☐ Were some funny?

☐ Select one and discuss how the message could have been sent straight.

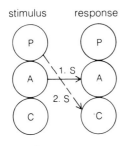

1. S:
2. S:

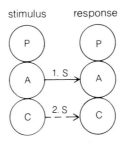

1. S:
2. S:

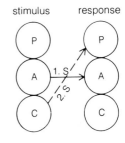

1. S:
2. S:

□ Bring it to school for a class art show.

□ For fun add some words of dialogue with a felt pen.

2 tv and ulterior messages

Analyze your favorite TV show.

□ Figure out which characters give what ulterior messages to each other and to the audience.

□ List at least three ulterior transactions and diagram them. (You might check out the commercials, too.)

3 essay on friendship

Look up the word *friendship* in the dictionary. Compare it with the word *love*. (Erich Fromm's *The Art of Loving* is a good resource.)

□ Write your own essay on the meaning of friendship.

suggested research

1 collage of ulterior transactions

Make a collage of ulterior looks and postures from magazines and newspapers.

15 ok and not-ok positions

case study 1 Harriet seemed to put herself down no matter how well she had done something. If she was complimented on a project that she'd turned in to a teacher, she would always say, "Well, that really isn't anything" or "If I could have had more time, it would have been better" or "You should see what Emily did." She felt so unsure of herself that she'd ask for directions over and over, not trusting her own feeling of what needed to be done next. Once she asked her English teacher seven times during a class period if she was on the right track with her essay. Her teacher finally became annoyed and cut her short. "Just go ahead and finish up your essay. You know what to do." Harriet felt rejected and went back to her seat pouting. It was a long time before she spoke to this teacher again. She remarked to her friends "Mr. Miller is the best English teacher in the school, but he sure doesn't like to help people."

case study 2 Harold often complained that he seemed to go "around in circles" and he wasn't getting anywhere. He was a mediocre student most of the way through school even though he was told by several of his teachers and counselors that he had much more ability than he seemed to use. Harold often cut class, did not complete assignments, and in general did not seem to get interested in anything that was going on in school. Harold also had a difficult time solving his problems at home. He often complained, "I just can't get along with my parents". All they do is push me around and they never help me with my homework". However, Harold didn't know how to improve his situation at school or at home.

psychological positions about self Children receive messages and have experiences which cause them to make decisions about themselves very early in life. These decisions become generalized into the basic OK and not-OK *psychological positions*.

Children who are physically neglected in early life suffer from disease or malnutrition. Children who are brutalized or constantly criticized are likely to begin early in life to de-value themselves. Eventually these kinds of children decide,

"I'm worthless," "I'm no good," "I don't deserve to live," "I make everyone else unhappy," "I'm stupid". Such decisions cause them to experience a general sense of being not OK, so they take an I'm not-OK psychological position.

Children who receive warm, affectionate care, good nutrition, appropriate protection, and who are treated with respect and accepted for what they are, develop a sense of confidence. If they also have reasonable limits set on their behavior and are encouraged to grow from dependency to independence, they are likely to respect themselves and make decisions about the self such as "I can do many things," "It's OK for me to be alive," "I can be somebody." Their early decisions give them a general sense of being OK. They take an I'm-OK psychological position.

Some people learn to feel OK about certain aspects of themselves but not-OK about other aspects of themselves. For example, they can feel physically attractive but intellectually stupid, mechanically inclined but socially misfits, brainy but not very masculine or feminine. Therefore, a personal sense of OK-ness varies with the situation. Not-OK feelings are usually part of the Adapted Child.

psychological positions about others

Children who experience other people as cold and aloof, critical and cruel, or angry and brutal, may decide, "People can't be trusted", "People are dangerous", "Other people are no good". As a result they take a You're not-OK psychological position about others.

In contrast, children who perceive their significant parent figures as strong, knowledgeable, loving and respectful, might eventually take such positions as "People are fair", "People can be trusted" "People will help me", "Other people know what to do". They thus assume a You're OK psychological position about others.

Sometimes the position a person takes about others is sexualized. For example, children who are brutalized by their fathers and rescued by their mothers may take the position that women are OK and men are not-OK. "All men are mean," "All women are nice and helpful." Children who find they can speak in confidence with their fathers but are continually criticized by their mothers, may decide, "You can trust men, but you can't trust women" or "Men are reasonable but women act too emotional." They thus take a psychological position that men are OK but women are not-OK.

the four basic psychological positions

Psychological positions about self and others provide a basic mind-set which motivates people to act in certain ways. The story of Fred may illustrate this. When Fred was very little he was given lots of attention and praise from his mother for learning to read early, learning to write his ABC's early, and for pleasing the teachers when he went to school. As a result, he learned to feel very confident about his mind and his academic ability.

However, his father mistrusted what he called "the academic type." He was very disappointed in his son because Fred was slight in build and not athletic. Over and over Fred was told, "After we practiced on you, we should have had another boy that would turn out to be a real man." Fred tried to become athletic in order to please his father and be accepted by him, but did not have the inherited physical abilities necessary for a star athlete. His father often kidded him, "You've got a better figure for being a girl."

Thus Fred felt OK about his academic abilities but very not-OK about his masculinity. He began to take undue risks when driving to make himself feel "tougher." He would take off in his car with tires screeching and speed down the street. In a sense, Fred was almost ready to kill himself in order to prove to his father and himself that he was "a real man".

Fred also took a negative position toward men and had a difficult time relating to his male teachers. He passed his tests and worked at a high level, but he felt angry at them much of the time. He also interpreted even a very reasonable assignment as an unfair demand.

As it does for all people, the psychological positions Fred had taken reflected how he felt about himself and how he felt about others. In turn, his feelings motivated him to behave in certain ways.

Here is how psychological positions may fit together:

First Position: I'm OK, You're OK. People with this position have a basic but realistic acceptance of the importance of people, including themselves. They can solve their problems constructively and what they expect from life is likely to be valid. This position is a mentally healthy position.

Second Position: I'm OK, You're not-OK. this position is taken by people who feel victimized or persecuted and consequently actually victimize and persecute others. People in this position blame others for their misery and may put them down or try to get rid of them. For example, they may force others away by humiliating or teasing them. Delinquents and criminals often have this position. Some become so extremely suspicious that they feel justified in robbing, brutalizing, or even killing.

Third Position: I'm not-OK, You're OK. This position is a common position of people who feel powerless when they compare themselves with others. They may try to get away from other people or may attach themselves like parasites to stronger people. In some cases this leads to psychological or physical depression, and in severe cases, to suicide.

The Fourth Position: I'm not-OK, You're not-OK. This position causes people to feel hopeless and lose interest in living. They mas act confused, severely depressed, irritated, and unpredictable. They may go around in circles never getting anywhere. In extreme cases they may commit suicide and/or homicide to get even or to escape.

position and attitudes about life	
a person who is in this position	feels this way about life
I'm OK, You're OK	Life is worth living. "Let's get on with it."
I'm OK, You're not-OK	Your life is are not worth much. "Get out of my way."
I'm not-OK, You're OK	My life is not worth much. "I'm nothing compared with you."
I'm not-OK, You're not-OK	Life is not worth anything at all. "There's no use."

You may have identified with more than one of these positions. Most people do.

Most people also act the positions in varying degrees of intensity. For example, someone in a "You're not-OK" position may give slight, indirect put-downs such as, "You look pretty good today. No wonder you didn't have a good time yesterday— you wore green," or "Well, if you wait long enough, and Jean doesn't get a better date, maybe you can go with her." Or the put-downs may be more serious, such as humiliating someone in public or beating someone up.

summary   In summary, children, as a result of their early life experiences, make decisions about their own worth and about the worth of other people. On the basis of these decisions, they take positions about themselves and others which are associated with feeling OK or not-OK. Later in life they reinforce the giving and getting of strokes to which they have become accustomed.

People who take *negative* positions about themselves tend later in life to collect negative feelings about themselves. People who take *positive* positions about themselves tend to collect and thus reinforce positive feelings about themselves for the rest of their lives. The same is true for the feelings people have toward others.

People can change their not-OK feelings. They can understand how they got them and can decide, using the Adult ego state, to do something to improve them. This includes learning how to reject not-OK messages that may be sent from others. People can also keep the OK feelings they already have. They can appreciate how they got them and how they contribute to their winning capacities.

exercises

1 evaluating case studies (group or individual)

Reread the case studies at the beginning of the unit (page 89) and discuss the following questions:

☐ What position was Harriet acting from? What makes you think so?

☐ What might have happened to her when she was a child that caused her to behave the way she did in a classroom?

☐ What position did Harold seem to be operating from?

☐ What might have happened to Harold as a child to cause him to act this way?

☐ How was he defeating himself with his behavior?

2 ok positions and behavior (group)

Discuss in small groups what a student might say and do in each of the positions listed:

I'm OK, You're OK

I'm OK, You're not-OK

I'm not-OK, You're OK

I'm not-OK, You're not-OK

☐ Now discuss what a teacher might say and do in each position.

☐ Last discuss what a parent might say and do in each position.

☐ What similarities and differences do you notice in the way you described students, teachers, and parents?

3 positions in friendship and marriage (group)

Take each position in turn. Discuss the kinds of friends and/or marriage partners that a person who operates frequently from each position would likely have.

I'm not-OK, You're OK

I'm OK, You're not-OK

I'm not-OK, You're not-OK

I'm OK, You're OK

suggested research

1 early decisions and behavior

Think of two important experiences that you had when you were a small child. (You may want to record this in your journal.)

☐ Now try to remember what you decided as a result of these experiences—both about yourself and about others.

☐ What position did you take such as I'm OK or I'm not-OK, and You're OK or You're not OK?

☐ Now see if you can relate this to anything that you do now.

☐ If you can, is this a negative force in your life? Or a positive force in your life?

☐ If the force resulting from the experience is negative, what can you do about it?

2 your sense of ok-ness

On a continuum from −10 to +10 rate how you feel about:

yourself most of the time.

−10 ——————————+———————————— +10

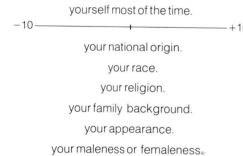

your national origin.

your race.

your religion.

your family background.

your appearance.

your maleness or femaleness.

How do you feel about people of:

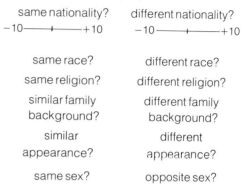

same nationality?	different nationality?
−10———+———+10	−10———+———+10
same race?	different race?
same religion?	different religion?
similar family background?	different family background?
similar appearance?	different appearance?
same sex?	opposite sex?

Are you aware of the reasons why you feel the way you feel about yourself? About others?

□ Now look at the positive (OK) and negative (not-OK) feelings that you indicated in each category.

□ Review each one and ask, "How does this feeling affect the way I behave?"

  □ Towards myself?

  □ Towards others?

□ What are three steps you could take to improve your attitudes about yourself and your attitudes about others?

16 the need for strokes

case study 1   Dwain "hurt all over", he wrote, "body, head, feelings, heart, all hurt . . . sick and tired of it all . . . no reason to go on . . . I'd be better off dead." The creative writing teacher had found the note crumpled in a waste basket. He'd never received it and couldn't quite remember who Dwain was until the despairing words jogged his memory. Dwain was the tall, skinny, pimply-faced sophomore who always seemed alone. He usually sat in a corner of the room by himself. When the teacher asked for volunteers to take parts or stage manage, Dwain consistently signed up for isolated jobs such as curtain pulling, which received little recognition.

case study 2   Joyce was quite the opposite. She had a bouncy personality and a great desire for recognition. When the drama teacher asked for volunteers, Joyce's hand was the first one up and inevitably she wanted to be sure her name was on the program. It always was. People responded to her warmth and her concern over others. Joyce was well liked.

case study 3   Oscar was a hard working, rather quiet student who would often volunteer for jobs requiring physical strength. Oscar could be counted on to do things such as moving scenery and arranging the auditorium. He carried his portable radio with him and was up on all sport events. Students and teachers occasionally stopped to ask him how some game was going. Oscar's face would light up and he would go into a long discussion of the ups and downs of the particular sports event.

introduction to strokes   According to Eric Berne, everyone structures time around "strokes." A stroke is a physical touch or a symbolic touch in the form of recognition. If a child does not receive sufficient strokes, growth—physiological, intellectual, and emotional—is impaired. In fact, an infant who receives almost no physical strokes will die.

Strokes are either positive or negative. Being hugged is a positive stroke; being spanked a negative one. If a person does not get *positive* strokes, he or she will do something to get negative strokes. Strokes are so necessary for survival that people prefer negative strokes to none at all.

Transactions are made up of strokes. The stimulus is one stroke, the response is another. Different people want different kinds of strokes. What feels good to one person may feel bad to another. Whereas one person might want a recognition stroke for hair style or clothes, another person might want a stroke for academic achievement, for prowess in sports or artistic endeavors.

Each ego state in each person may want different kinds of strokes. Since each person's ego states are different, each person's Parent, Adult, and Child will look for different strokes. The stroke needs of two students might be as follows:

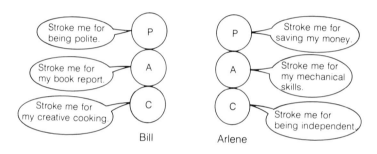

Bill   Arlene

strokes for the Child   The strokes a person wants for the Child ego state are related to the strokes he or she received in childhood. A child who is cuddled and handled a lot, who receives praise and recognition in early childhood will continue to expect them in later life and know how to get them.

In contrast, a person who receives lots of negative put-downs or physical abuse in childhood will continue to expect similar strokes later and know how to get them. Whereas a person who gets positive strokes usually will anticipate more of the same kind of pleasurable strokes, a person who gets negative strokes will later anticipate hurtful strokes—either physical or verbal.

People who are isolated and who receive minimal strokes in childhood are likely to expect similar isolation and the absence of strokes later in life. They may also be unable to stroke others, acting distant and indifferent when excitement or enthusiasm would be more appropriate. Yet strokes are necessary and everyone needs to get them and give them.

You can become aware of your Child needs for positive verbal strokes by remembering your childhood and the best thing ever said to you. If nothing positive was said, then remember what you *wished* people would say to you when you were little. You can also become aware of your Child needs for nonverbal strokes by remembering the kinds of touching (*e.g.*, a back rub) that felt especially good to you. Or the things that were done for you (*e.g.*, a birthday party) that felt especially good. When people grow up they continue to hope for the pleasurable things that happened to them, or that they wish had happened to them in childhood.

strokes for the Parent   The strokes one wants for one's Parent ego state are similar to the kinds of strokes one's own parents wanted. If a person's parents wanted people to be mannerly and polite, to say "please" and "thank you," then that person will expect the same kinds of polite strokes from others.

You can become aware of your Parent stroke needs by remembering your childhood and the things that pleased your parents (*e.g.*, good grades, a clean house, being punctual). These same things may please the Parent ego state in you now. In other words, part of you will want what your parent figures wanted.

strokes for the Adult   The main function of the Adult is to take in information, to compute the information rationally, and to give it out or act on the basis of it. Therefore, the kinds of strokes the Adult needs are quite different from those the Parent or Child need.

Seemingly, the main need of the Adult is to have the chance to function smoothly so that it doesn't get rusty as fine machinery often will if it is not used. By functioning well, the Adult gets self-stroking.

However, if the Adult is not recognized by others, the Child in the person may become resentful and may motivate the Adult to push to get strokes of recognition. In its most interesting form this is happening in the current women's movement. More and more women are asking for Adult recognition for their rational thinking skills. They as well as men have become aware of the second-class citizen roles women have played historically. They resent that the focus has been mostly on their nurturing abilities and feminine charms while so little attention has been given to their thinking abilities and skills. New federal legislation and the number of affirmative action programs for women reflect an increasing concern for this.

The opposite emphasis is happening in some parts of the male world. Historically, men have been stroked for their Adult thinking. However, more and more men are asking for fun strokes for their Child. For example, the brighter colors currently being worn by men are like invitations to be noticed. Furthermore, many men are taking jobs that call for nurturing others, such as male nursing and social work. Many men are also taking a more open nurturing role by being more active in rearing children and caring for them.

You can become aware of your Adult stroke needs by considering your thinking processes and skills. If you are getting recognition from others for using your intelligence, then you are getting strokes for your Adult. If you are not, then you may not be showing this side of your personality to other people.

strokes in friendship   Friendships usually develop because the two people involved use complementary transactions that provide the positive strokes each person expects. They laugh together, Child to Child. They study together, Adult to Adult. They baby-sit together, Parent to Parent. They ask for and receive help, Child to Parent. In close relationships people can verbalize their stroke needs to each other and can practice giving the positive kinds of strokes that help each other feel like a winner.

Some people actually feel good to be around; they send out good "vibes." Others are uncomfortable to be around; they send out bad "vibes." The difference is often in the kind of strokes they give out and the kind they'll take. Some people are good at expressing their warm appreciative feelings towards others. Some are very poor at it. Everyone can learn how to do it better. Good friends often stroke one another positively:

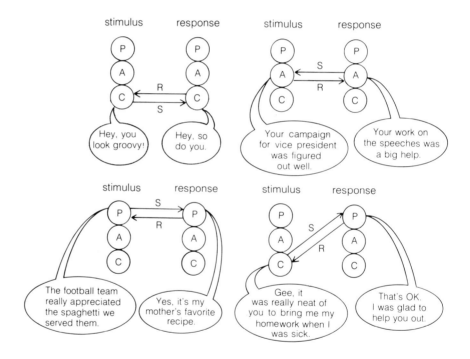

strokes and marriage   One of the reasons people are attracted to each other is because their negative and positive stroke needs and their abilities to give negative and positive strokes seem to mesh. If stroke needs mesh, like gears in a car, two people are likely to stay together a long time.

All couples have to figure out what kinds of strokes each partner appreciates most. For example, Susan's mother always gave her tea and custard when Susan was ill. This seemed to make her feel better. Her husband's mother, however, always fixed milk toast when he was ill.

When Susan became ill shortly after their marriage, her husband fixed her milk toast and she broke out in tears. Later she was able to figure out that this wasn't the kind of stroke that made her fell better and asked her husband to fix custard and tea next time.

Susan's husband felt bad when she didn't like the milk toast he'd fixed for her. His intentions were good but he gave the kind of stroke he would have liked rather than what Susan liked. However, he was happy to change when he saw how important it was to her and understood that she wasn't putting him down.

Many people want specific strokes if they feel down. Some want sympathy, some want a sense of "I'm on your team." Others want approval or shared laughter. Each has unique stroke needs. Giving and getting the hoped-for positive stroke adds to a happy relationship.

intensity of strokes Strokes are experienced at different levels of intensity. For example, the word "hello" is a single stroke that can be said casually and is, therefore, a minimal maintenance stroke. "Hello" can also be said with some intensity. The word will then carry feelings at a deeper level.

Some people give and receive only superficial maintenance strokes. Winners choose relationships and strokes that are at a deeper level and, therefore, more intense and longer lasting.

summary In summary, negative strokes, either verbal or nonverbal, diminish a person's self-esteem. The more intense they are, the more they hurt and the longer they are remembered. Positive strokes are usually the kind of transactions that are direct, appropriate, and relevant to the situation. When strokes are positive, they leave people feeling good, alive, alert, and significant. At a greater depth, they enhance people's sense of well-being, endorse their intelligence, and are often pleasurable to experience. Positive strokes include feelings of goodwill and convey the I'm-OK, you're-OK position. Stroking that is authentic, honest, and not overdone actually nourishes people. Their winning streaks are expanded.

The awareness of stroke needs is a healthy development both within an individual and within society. Stroke needs can be met.

exercises

1 evaluating case studies (group or individual)

Reread the case studies at the beginning of the unit (page 95) and answer the following questions:

☐ What kind of strokes do you think Dwain needed that he didn't get?

☐ What could he have done differently to get strokes?

☐ What kind of strokes might a friend give Dwain?

☐ What ego state in Joyce got the most strokes?

☐ Was it a pattern? If so, why?

☐ What strokes did Oscar get for his ego states?

☐ Do you think all his ego state stroke needs were met? If so, why? If not, why not?

2 giving positive and negative strokes (group)

Sit in a circle and have each person give the person on the left a negative stroke. After going around the circle discuss how you felt when getting the negative stroke and how you felt when giving one.

☐ What ego state gave the stroke?

☐ What ego state received the stroke?

Now repeat the process, giving each person a positive stroke. Discuss how you felt when getting the positive stroke and how you felt when giving one.

☐ What ego state gave the stroke?

☐ What ego state received the stroke?

3 your favorite strokes (individual)

On the right side of your ego state portrait, list two favorite positive strokes for each of your ego states. On the left side, list two negative strokes for each ego state.

negative strokes   positive strokes

☐ How does the awareness of the negative and positive strokes make you *feel* in your Child?

☐ What does your Adult *think* about the strokes?

☐ What are your Parent *opinions* about the strokes?

4 favorite strokes when feeling down (group)

Think of times when you were little and were sick, hurt, or humiliated.

☐ Share with your group what was done for you that you liked.

☐ Discuss why this made you feel better.

☐ Discuss if you expect anything like this from your friends now.

□ Be aware of how you *feel* about their response.

□ Write a brief paper about your experience.

2 strokes and relationships

Write down the names of three people—a parent figure, a friend, a neighbor.

□ Guess at the strokes each of their ego states might want. Record them in your journal as shown.

parent
figure   friend   neighbor

P ———— P ———— P ————
A ———— A ———— A ————
C ———— C ———— C ————

□ As soon as possible go ask them or observe them more closely to see how accurate you were.

suggested research

1 hello again

Try an experiment for one day. In each of your classes or in your neighborhood, say "hello" to several people you usually ignore.

□ Observe their response to this stroke from you.

part four

17 collecting psychological trading stamps

case study 1 Luanne was described as "moody" by her friends. Her feelings were hurt easily, although generally she did not show it. Instead, she built up resentment until she felt really down and depressed. Every so often she would stay home with a "sick headache," feeling sorry for herself. Luanne had decorated her room in dark, somber colors, and when she was in one of her down moods, she'd close herself off in her room. She felt justified in withdrawing from other people this way because "the way people treat me depresses me."

case study 2 Charlie was described by his friends as "unpredictable." He seemed to be even-tempered much of the time, yet suddenly and, as it seemed to his friends, without any warning he would blow up. Something seemed to smolder inside Charlie that he never handled well. Instead he would suddenly erupt, venting his anger on the people near him. For example, if he got a no from his parents or girl friend, he sometimes accepted it calmly. At other times, however, Charlie would yell back in irrational anger. In school his behavior was usually acceptable, but his record showed that he had banged in a wall with his fist on four different occasions. A close friend said Charlie was like a volcano. "When he lets go, watch out!"

case study 3 When Millie was little, she often overheard her mother complaining, "I almost died when Millie was born, and I still suffer from it." In school Millie often sat looking down at the floor with her legs tightly crossed. She spoke softly and with great hesitation as if she were weighing every word. When her counselor commented on this, Millie broke into tears and between sobs stammered out, "I'm sorry, it seems like I always do everything wrong. All my life, it seems like everything is my fault."

case study 4 Martin liked himself. It showed in the way he walked and the way he talked. For years he had been active in the 4-H club and now as a senior, having won many awards for his livestock, Martin headed toward college with a scholarship that would fully pay his expenses for two years. Although he was the strong silent type who didn't talk much, Martin was often surrounded by a group of close friends who had similar interests.

introduction to psychological trading stamps

Have you ever noticed how some people seem to ask for negative strokes by setting themselves up to be put down? Some people get mad but hold it in until they "can't take it any longer" and then blow up. Others always seem to act apologetically when things go wrong and make remarks such as "It's all my fault" even when it isn't. Still other people seem to go from one success to another, acting as though they feel good about themselves and giving out positive "vibes" that imply "I'm OK and so are you."

In TA the good or bad feelings a person collects are called "psychological trading stamps." The term *stamps* is borrowed from the practice in some parts of the country of collecting trading stamps when making purchases and later redemming them for merchandise.[7] Collecting a good feeling from a positive stroke is collecting a *psychological gold stamp*. Collecting a bad feeling from a negative stroke is collecting a *psychological gray stamp*.

Sometimes a specific color is assigned to a stamp to represent a bad feeling: red stamps for anger, blue stamps for hurt feelings and depression, white stamps for purity and self-righteousness, and green stamps for jealousy and envy. The color assigned to stamps is not as important as the fact that psychological trading stamps represent a state in which people indulge in feelings learned in childhood. These feelings are then saved up and eventually "redeemed."

You've probably heard the word *overindulgence*. People overindulge themselves with food, drink, drugs, clothes, or TV. They also do so with feelings and the behavior that results from them. People can actually overindulge themselves in feelings of anger, hurt, guilt, or depression.

Psychological stamp collecting is common. Everyone does it from time to time.

stamp collections and childhood feelings

People are not born with their feelings already programed toward objects and people. They learn who the people are toward whom they can show affection. They learn toward whom and about what to feel guilty. They learn whom and what to fear. They learn whom and what to hate. They learn how to give and receive certain kinds of strokes in order to give and receive certain kinds of feelings.

When children are very young they experience many different feelings. Eventually, however, each child learns to respond with specific feelings which become favorites. These feelings are the beginning of the stamp collection. Often these feelings are inappropriate to the later occasion or the person to which they are applied, because they are responses to past experiences rather than to the present situation.

For example, children who continually hear, "I'm ashamed of you!" or "You should be ashamed of yourself!" learn to collect guilt stamps. As teenagers they often feel guilty if something goes wrong.

Children who continually hear, "Just wait until your father gets home. He'll beat you with a board!" learn to collect fear stamps. They may grow up feeling afraid of men or think of men as *the* authority figures.

Children who continually hear, "Don't speak to those people! They can't be trusted" learn to collect suspicion stamps. As grownups they will be suspicious of people who are different from themselves.

Children who continually hear, "What's the matter with you! Can't you do anything right!" learn to collect stupid stamps. They are likely to grow up feeling stupid and goof up on many things. Or they may think they have to be perfect all the time and feel stupid at the slightest mistake.

Children who often hear, "You've got a good mind, you can figure it out," learn to trust themselves. They grow up feeling confident and good about themselves and usually do the best they can with what they have. They tend to use their Adult ego state to think things through.

Children who continually hear, "I love you and I'm glad you're you" will learn to feel comfortable about being who they are and will probably feel the same way when they've grown up.

These feelings are learned responses to the original childhood situations. The problem comes, however, when the feelings learned are negative. Later in life, people tend to seek out situations in which they get a particular stroke so that they can *re-experience the old negative feelings*. They do this not because they want to feel negative but because they need strokes, and negative strokes of recognition are better than none, just as bad food is better than none when one is hungry. These old feelings are saved up as psychological trading stamps. A person who in childhood takes the position "I'm stupid", later collects feelings of stupidity from several situations and then feels justified in doing something dumb. "After all, what can you expect from me. I have no brains! And I want strokes for that."

People may also learn to give negative strokes to others perhaps by acting self-righteously and feeling pious about themselves (collecting white stamps for purity).

People who unknowingly need to add to their own collections of negative feelings, do this by manipulating others in order to hurt them, belittle them, anger them, frighten them, arouse their guilt, or reject them. They provoke or invite others to put them down.

Put-downs needn't be real, they can even be imagined. For example, Millie *imagined* her teacher was mad at her when actually her teacher was frowning because of a headache. An imagined put-down is like a *counterfeit stamp*, yet it has the same negative effect as a real put-down, and feels like a negative stroke.

cashing in negative trading stamps

When people save up their negative feelings they eventually cash them in for a prize. The prize is what they feel entitled to. For example, some people who don't get their way feel entitled to act confused. Others feel entitled to get angry, still others may get depressed. People who are confused, who get angry, depressed and so forth may redeem their stamps by doing such things as getting sick, flunking a test, striking out at someone, pouting, and brooding. They feel justified in this because they have "taken so much" and resent it. The process is:

Collecting stamps ⟶ growing resentment ⟶ cashing in for a psychological prize

People acquire collections of different sizes and have different compulsions as to when, where, and how to redeem their collections. Some people have small collections and only cash in every once in a while for relatively small prizes such as having a headache, throwing an eraser, yelling at someone, or having a temper tantrum.

For some people, however, the prize is bigger. If they have saved several "books" of negative stamps, they may feel justified in doing such things as injuring themselves, freaking out on drugs, stealing someone else's property, getting drunk, breaking up with a good friend, or losing a job.

Occasionally people spend years and save up an even larger collection. They then cash it in for a grand prize: mental breakdown, imprisonment, dropping out of society, and in extreme cases, homicide, or suicide.

When people feel they have collected enough negative stamps and are ready to cash them in, certain words and phrases are likely to be used to indicate that redemption time is at hand. You've probably heard one of these:

"Nobody around here cares. I'm going to leave."

"That's the last straw!"

"I never do anything right. I'm not going to try anymore."

"I've taken all I can take."

cashing in positive trading stamps

Instead of getting and giving negative feelings, some people learn to get and give good feelings. Their collection of positive feelings includes being pleasant, helpful, interesting, responsive, good at something, and fun to be with. This behavior encourages others to respond positively with smiles, compliments, trust, and caring behavior, thus giving them more good feelings.

People draw on their store of positive feelings, and when they've collected enough, they feel justified in doing something good for themselves. They may cash in their small collections of gold stamps by going out to dinner, buying a new shirt, having a fun weekend, or taking a pleasant vacation.

Since the size of the collection determines the size of the prize, people with medium-size collections have more joy out of life then those with smaller collections. Instead of an occasional small treat, they feel justified in cashing in for some larger prizes such as applying for a scholarship award, getting a good volunteer or paying job, finding a new friend, or volunteering help for a political candidate.

Some people gather even larger collections of gold stamps. Being a gold stamp collector doesn't only mean having a good time. It also means long-term planning and working toward a chosen goal. One may study hard in college for the special gold stamps at graduation. Another may work hard at a sculpture and then stand back and collect lots of good feelings over the finished product. Another practices diligently playing a favorite instrument, collecting many gold stamps as he/she gets proficient at it.

Having a large gold stamp collection enables people to return a lot of gold stamps to others. Such people care about others and show it by smiling, listening, sharing, and being open. They do not feel threatened at the success of others.

People who collect good feelings about themselves and others are able to cope with serious difficulties. They often come up smiling, even on the gray days.

When a person feels she or he has collected enough *positive* stamps and is ready to cash them in, certain words and phrases are often used to indicate that redemption time is at hand:

"Now it's time for some fun. Let's have a party."

"Let's go to the beach for the weekend."

"I'm going to work for an A and I bet I get it."

"I know I'll get that job. I'm ready for it."

People who learn to feel OK about themselves and others have learned to give and receive positive strokes. They direct their energies toward the kind of behavior that gives them positive feelings of joy, competence, and confidence. They are gold stamp collectors. They are winners.

trading stamps and relationships

Friends may be used to provoke situations that help people collect their favorite feelings, positive or negative. For example, Suzie fixed a great picnic lunch. Her friend, Mary, wanted to give her a gold stamp by complimenting her on it. Instead of accepting the gold stamp (which is collecting good feelings about herself), Suzie replied, "Gee, it really wasn't anything. I only had 45 minutes." Thus she collected a gray stamp instead of gold. Mary also felt bad because her compliment was refused and she was put down. Thus she collected a gray stamp for herself.

People often cash in their stamps on those who are in an authority position relative to them. For example, George was often angry at his teachers but never talked over his problems with any of them. Instead, he manipulated them by writing so sloppily that they'd criticize him. He then collected pages of anger stamps which he carried home and cashed in on his younger sister. George was not aware that he had learned in childhood to get angry with his parents, hold it in and never talk to them about it, and then vent his anger on someone he saw as "weaker" than himself.

Friends are also used when cashing in positive stamp collections. After passing an important exam, good friends may celebrate with a night out at the movies, a picnic, a shopping spree, or some other way of doing something good for themselves. Friends who are gold stamp collectors often reinforce the confidence, competence, and growth of one another.

summary   In summary, people learn negative and positive feelings in childhood. These feelings become part of their identity, and later in life, often without knowing it, they collect these same feelings. Such feelings become their negative or positive stamp collection. These collections are saved up in different amounts by different people. They are cashed in either with negative or with positive behavior. Learning to be a winner means giving up your negative collection in favor of feeling good about yourself and others.

exercises

1 evaluating case studies (group or individual)

Review the case studies at the beginning of the unit (pp. 104-105) and answer the following questions for each one:

What seemed to be the person's favorite feeling to collect?

How might he/she have learned this pattern?

What was her/his method of cashing in?

2 giving and receiving feelings (group)

Read over the following two situations. Discuss at least three examples of how bad feelings could be given by one person and collected by someone else.

A teacher returns an essay with a low grade because the handwriting is bad and there are three misspelled words.

A student doesn't make it home on time. Dinner is cold and most of the choice morsels have been eaten.

☐ Now discuss how better feelings might have been given by one person and collected by someone else in each of these situations.

☐ Select one of the above situations or design your own. Role play the situation, first giving and collecting negative feelings, next giving and receiving positive feelings.

3 counterfeit stamps (group)

Reread the comment on counterfeit stamps (see page 106). Think of ways these kinds of stamps could be collected around school. Also, think of ways they might be given—even

unknowingly. Be prepared to share your group's ideas with the rest of the class.

suggested research

1 your negative stamp collection

Try to recall at least two situations in the last week in which you collected and held on to a negative feeling.

☐ What was the situation?

☐ Who was involved?

☐ What feeling(s) did you collect?

☐ Do you still hold resentment over either or both of these situations?

☐ When you have taken enough from people, how do you cash in? Whom or what do you cash in on?

☐ Now explore alternatives to taking it. Could you have handled the situation a different way so that you didn't collect?

☐ Try to discover any pattern of stamp collecting and redeeming you have learned from your past experiences that may be a hindrance to you now.

☐ You may want to record some of your findings in your journal.

2 your gold stamp collection

Recall at least two situations during the past two weeks in which you received positive strokes and collected gold stamps.

☐ What was the situation?

□ Who was involved?

□ How did you feel?

□ Does the memory of it make you feel good now?

□ What good things do you do for yourself when you cash in gold stamps?

3 people and stamps

Make a list of four people who are close to you—relatives, friends, etc.

□ What kinds of negative stamps do you give and receive from each?

□ What kinds of positive stamps do you give and receive from each?

Person	Negative Stamps Given and Received	Positive Stamps Given and Received

□ After you have studied the list, figure out what you would like to change?

□ How could you do it?

18 theory of games people play

case study 1 Milt was a pleasant, affable sophomore who usually received poor grades for his academic work because he seldom turned in his assignments. Two weeks before report-card time Milt would regularly approach his teachers and ask if he could make up his work. Suggestions were often made that he could do extra reading and book reports to improve his grade. However, Milt was never willing to do so. He continually turned down the suggestions with remarks such as "Yes, but I haven't time," or "Yes, but I don't have the right books," or "Yes, but I don't really understand what I'm supposed to do."

case study 2 Mrs. Taka obviously cared about her students. She was willing to meet with them during her lunch period, before or after school. When Milt asked for make-up work so he could get a better grade, she suggested what he could do and how he could do it. When he said yes, but he could not get the book, she replied, "Why don't you use my copy?" When he said yes, but he didn't have enough time, she offered, "Why don't you take an extra week to prepare the report." When he replied, "Yes, but I need at least ten days," she suggested, "Why don't you try to have it handed in to me in eight days?" On the due date, the report wasn't ready. "Yes," lamented Milt, "but I just couldn't understand it." Mrs. Taka felt angry and frustrated and made no further suggestions to Milt.

case study 3 Debby was cute. Her friends agreed that there was no doubt about it. When Debby tossed her long hair back over her shoulders, rolled her eyes flirtatiously, smiled at others, and spoke to them with animation, people around seemed to sparkle in response. However, although Debby attracted all the new students that came to City High, they didn't seem to stay attracted to her long. After a couple of conversations or dates, each one would drift away. As Tom explained it, "She may be good looking but who needs to listen to her complaining all the time. I get enough of that verbal garbage laid on me by my brother." Debby was aware that she lost her friends easily, that people who first seemed to like her later seemed to avoid her, but she didn't know what to do about it.

case study 4   Ken was slow moving and was left-handed. He was often called stupid by the other members of his family when they tried to get him to use his right hand instead of his left hand. He heard many times, "Why can't you do anything right, stupid." When Ken entered school he had a difficult time learning to read and often acted clumsily. The school psychologist thought his intelligence was normal, and that his reading problem was emotional. Ken felt confused in school, dropped out in the tenth grade commenting to his home room teacher, "I'm just too dumb to get all this."

introduction to psychological games   Do you know someone who often gets picked on by others? Do you know anyone who seems to spend a lot of time picking on others or putting others down? Do you know someone who intervenes when others are having problems and tries to rescue them? If you have seen such people, then you've seen them playing the basic roles in psychological games — Victim, Persecutor, and Rescuer.

Games are defined as a series of complementary transactions with a hidden motive which leads to a payoff. This hidden motive is experienced as an ulterior transaction. A game usually ends up with someone feeling not-OK. This feeling is the psychological payoff for playing the game. Game players seldom know they're into a game, even though they are making the same moves over and over again, often with the same people.

The psychological games people play are similar in some ways to games played when people get together socially. Someone starts the game. If the other players know their correct moves, the game proceeds to a predictable ending. The difference between social games and psychological games is that psychological games are not played for fun. Usually someone gets put down, maybe even hurt. For example, a person in a Victim role reexperiences a Child feeling of I'm not-OK. A person playing Rescuer or Persecutor reinforces the You're not-OK feelings.

Game roles are phoney roles. They are play-acted in response to early childhood experiences rather than to present situations. However, persecutor, victim, and rescuer functions are *legitimate* if the people involved are not play-acting or getting some kind of secret satisfaction out of it, but are behaving in ways that are appropriate to the present situation. Examples of legitimate functioning are:

persecutors: People who set necessary limits on behavior or are charged with enforcing a rule and are perceived as persecuting.

victims: People who qualify for a job but are denied it because of race, sex, or religion.

rescuers: People helping others who are functioning inadequately to rehabilitate themselves and to stand on their own two feet.

When these roles are like masks, they are *illegitimate* and used for purposes of manipulation. Subsequently, when these three words are capitalized they refer to

113

the manipulative, illegitimate roles that people act out as part of their psychological games.

Persecutors: People who set unnecessarily strict limits on behavior; who enforce rules with sadistic brutality; who make others suffer because they are weaker.

Victims: People who do *not* qualify for a job but falsely claim they are denied it because of race, sex, or religion.
People who feel continually put upon.

Rescuers: People who, in the guise of being helpful, keep others dependent upon them, don't really help them and in fact may resent helping.

Phoney roles are always part of a game.

how games begin People learn to play specific games because of negative childhood experiences. For example, a little girl who is called Stupid learns to think of herself as stupid. She may later in life act stupid, even though she has a good mind. She is also likely to play the game of *Stupid*. This was true of a senior student who assisted in an office three afternoons a week. She often reproduced the wrong reports, delayed important mail, sent messages to the wrong offices, and did "stupid" things. Other people were exasperated and often provoked into calling her "stupid". Eventually this student managed to get herself fired, which was a losing way to behave not only because she needed her job for the money, but because the job gave her self-respect. In her personal life she also lost because she went with a young man who exploited her, used her car, borrowed money he never paid back, and who dropped her when she lost her job. A *Stupid* player usually ends up in the role of Victim and finds someone else to respond in the role of Persecutor or the role of Rescuer.

Another student also choosing a Victim role might play a different game, such as *Look How Hard I'm Trying*. This game, like *Stupid*, is developed in childhood as a response to parents who demand perfection. People who play it try and try and try but never get full approval from others and end up feeling like a Victim. They thus reexperience the strokes and the feeling they had when they were little — always trying, never doing it quite right. In each case they confirm the initial I'm not-OK position.

the yes, but game Have you ever found yourself in a situation in which someone asked you for help with a problem but didn't really want it? Perhaps you gave them all kinds of advice and ideas to try. Yet every time you gave that person an idea, your idea was rejected. If so, you were caught up in a game of *Yes, But*.

This is a very common game. The person who learned it in childhood decided — with good reason at the time — to resent authority figures. When the game is played later in life, the feeling underneath is still resentment against authorities — whether critical or nurturing, and the game is played to put them off. *Yes, But* is also played to delay taking action, making decisions, or solving problems. In other words, it's an adaptation from childhood which to some people justifies their procrastinating indefinitely. They tell others their problems, reject their advice, and thus delay solving the problems.

The person who starts a game is called "It". In the game of *Yes, But,* the first move is made when the person who is It tells someone else that she or he has a problem. The second move occurs when the other person with the complementary hand gives ideas, solutions, or advice. The initial *Yes, But* player, however, does not really want advice; every time advice is given, he or she finds some way to reject it or put it down. On the surface the transaction is a plausible Adult to Adult transaction in which the problem is stated in such a way that it sounds genuine. However, the hidden transaction in the game is something else. It's a put-off.

The ego states involved in the game of *Yes, But* can be diagramed. In the illustration the solid lines, Adult-Adult, indicate the plausible, surface transaction. The dotted lines, Child-Parent, indicate the hidden ulterior transaction.

stimulus   response

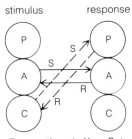

Transactions in *Yes, But*

The actual dialogue might go like this:

Surface Transaction

Adult — Adult

1. Friend: "You see, I have this problem. I really don't seem to be able to get my mother to listen to me."

2. Friend: "Well, why don't you tell your mother you'd like her to listen to you."

1. Friend: "Well, yes, I could try that, but my mother can't even pay attention long enough for me to tell her I need her to listen."

2. Friend: "Why don't you go home tonight and tell her that you want to talk to her later; you know, sort of make an appointment."

1. Friend: "Well, yes, but she's always so busy that trying to make an appointment with her is worse than going to the dentist."
(And on, and on, and on.)

The hidden meaning might be as follows:

Ulterior Transaction

Child — Parent and Parent — Child

1. Friend: "Poor Me. Just try to help me."

2. Friend: "Here's my help. See how helpful I am?"

1. Friend: "Not enough. Try harder."

2. Friend: "OK, I'm trying."

1. Friend: "You don't even have as much information as I do. And anyway, I don't want your help."

2. Friend: Goes away feeling defeated and put off.

The game ends at an impasse when It wins the game because the other player runs out of advice. It, who starts out acting like a Victim, switches to Persecutor and eventually makes the other person feel inadequate about giving solutions. The second player, who started out acting like a Rescuer, then becomes the Victim, feeling bad and thinking something like, "Gee, I was only trying to help you."

Since one of the reasons people play games is to collect their stamps, each receives their payoffs — their favorite feeling.

rapo

Have you ever noticed how some people seem to give others a come-on and then when they get the expected response, brush them off? If so, you've seen the game of *Rapo*.

For example, if one student flirts with another, gets a positive response, then refuses further advances, the game is likely to be *Rapo*. In the game of *Rapo* the surface transactions seem honest. However, there is an ulterior transaction, Child to Child. It is often nonverbal such as batting eyelashes, a knowing grin, or a phoney smile. "Say, aren't you new around here?" said with a flirty look could be a come-on. If the new person is hooked and then brushed off, a game has likely been played. In a classical game of *Rapo* the game ends when the person who initiated the game feels innocent and justified in being angry because of the sexual advances made by the other person.

The game of *Rapo* can be played between people of opposite sexes or people of the same sex. It does not always have a sexual undertone. The same dynamics are working whenever there is a come-on followed by a brush-off. This happens when one person comes on friendly, then rejects the other person who responds in friendship. The complementary game of the second player is likely to be *Stupid* or another game called *Kick Me*. In both these games one person inflicts the put-down and the other accepts being put down and feels vaguely guilty.

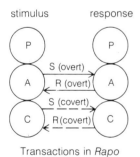

stimulus   response

Transactions in *Rapo*

summary

In summary, people play games for many reasons: to reinforce their psychological positions of I'm not-OK and/or You're not-OK which they learned in childhood; to get the strokes they are used to; to justify their indulging in collecting, giving out, or cashing in their negative stamp collections; to avoid getting too close to people; to fill up their time; to keep from solving problems; and to delay making changes.

Losers use a lot of their time playing games. Learning to be a winner means becoming aware of games and learning to break them up in favor of more honest and less hurtful transactions.

exercises

1 evaluating case studies (group or individual)

Reread the case studies at the beginning of the unit (pp. 112-113) and answer the following questions:

☐ What kind of roles did Milt tend to play with his teachers?

☐ What did Milt do that was ulterior?

☐ What game roles was Mrs. Taka involved in?

☐ How did Debby attract people and then put them off?

☐ What game roles did Debby play? How might others feel who get caught in her game pattern?

☐ How did Ken's early life experience affect his behavior in school?

☐ Discuss some of the facial expressions, postures, and gestures that Ken might begin to use in order to act out his life drama.

2 game roles people play (groups of three)

Take the game roles of Victim, Persecutor, and Rescuer, and act out a teacher/student situation.

3 role-playing *yes, but* (group)

In groups of three or four persons review the game of *Yes, But*. Then prepare to act out the game.

☐ The player who is selected to be It presents a problem to the others. The problem can be real or hypothetical.

□ The rest of the group then gives advice and solutions.

□ The person who is It cuts these ideas down.

□ The process continues until It feels glee at having put off the other player who in turn feel frustrated because help wasn't really wanted.

suggested research

1 games in the comic strip

Comic strips often show ulterior transactions. They may even show a final payoff which indicates a game.

□ Pick one of your favorite comics and diagram the transactions.

□ Did any of these transactions indicate a game?

2 game roles in the newspaper

Look through the newspaper.

□ Choose one article that reflects *legitimate* victim, persecutor, or rescuer situations.

□ Choose another article for possible game roles.

□ Identify the transactions and the games that might be played in the situation.

□ Do you think the newspaper reporter was playing any games? If so, what kind?

19 games played to get put-downs

case study 1   George was a junior in high school. He did a lot of complaining about how people treated him and how hard it was for him to make it in the "system". George rarely turned homework in on time. He had developed a habit of letting everything go until the last minute and then frantically trying to get in the assignments he needed to pass the course. At the end of his junior year it was questionable whether or not he would start the next year as a senior.

case study 2   Rosa tried very hard to do everything perfectly. She was a college preparatory student of average intelligence. However, she frequently worried, took books home every night to study, and sometimes cried bitterly when she could not understand a problem or complete an assignment. Though her transcript looked good — it had mainly B's and a few A's — Rosa did not feel good about it. She felt like a failure. No matter what she did, she never thought it was good enough. Consequently, Rosa spent much of her time worrying about what might happen to her and her grades when she went on to college.

case study 3   Howard's parents were killed in an auto accident when he was five years old. He then went to live in a large gloomy house with two unmarried aunts who seldom smiled. As Howard grew up he frequently felt very depressed. In spite of his innate ability to achieve success, he often withdrew to his room muttering, "I just can't make it" and "Why does everything always happen to me?" The school psychologist was concerned about the signs of Howard's increasing depression and withdrawal and helped Howard find professional help.

case study 4   Sarah and Alice were fraternal twins and good friends — usually. However, trouble would periodically flare up between them over the subject of boys. Sarah was not as attractive as Alice, but was more fun. Alice had a better figure but not as friendly a personality. Some boys preferred Sarah, some preferred Alice, and the girls had an agreement not to flirt with each other's "property." Alice frequently broke the agreement, and when she did, Sarah would refuse to talk to her for days.

introduction to victim games

Have you seen people who act dumb and then feel bad if anyone calls them stupid? Have you seen people who can't organize their time, who arrive late, who constantly do things that make other people mad? Have you seen people who seem to set themselves up so that later they will be depressed? If so, you have seen people playing games to get themselves put down. Once again they can collect a negative stamp.

The game of *Kick Me* requires a Victim looking for a "kick" and a Persecutor who is willing to do the kicking. In a mild form of the game the kick could be a dirty look; in a more serious game, the kick could be a beating. It's hard to believe, but it's true that some people get their kicks out of being hurt.

In the game of *Kick Me* the player does something to provoke put-downs.

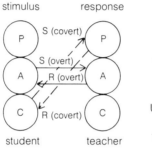

Surface Transaction: Adult-Adult

Student: I stayed up too late last night and didn't get my report finished.

Teacher: Today is the last day for reports to be turned in. You'll have to take a lower grade.

Ulterior Transaction: Child-Parent, Parent-Adult

Student: I've been bad; kick me.

Teacher: OK. Here's your kick.

The game of *Stupid* is similar to *Kick Me*. The kick, however, is related to the person's intelligence. "How could you do such a dumb thing!" is a frequent end to the game, with the other person feeling inadequate and stupid.

cops and robbers

In the game of *Cops and Robbers* one player tries to get away with something, the second player catches the first "in the act" or "with the goods". When this is a game the "robber" always gets caught and thus ends up the Victim — in the principal's office, juvenile hall, or jail. The principal, probation officer, or jailer is seen as the "cop" — the Persecutor. On the surface level, *Cops and Robbers* appears as a battle of wits. However, the ulterior transaction is different. Actually, the game is not a battle of wits. It is really like young children playing hide and seek. Those who are not found do something obvious, insisting on being caught. A characteristic of this kind of "robber" is leaving clues around that range from love letters to fingerprints.

courtroom

Cops and Robbers often leads to a three-handed game of *Courtroom*. In this game, the "plaintiff" and "the defendant", both competing for the Victim role, appeal to a "judge" to pass sentence, finding one person right and the other person wrong. If the judge takes sides, then he or she is going to be seen as a Persecutor by the one who loses the case and as a Rescuer by the one who's "not guilty."

In a family, this game is often played between quarreling children and an intervening parent. At school, it may be played between two students with a teacher or a third student acting as judge and jury.

Mary: You had no business making eyes at Bill while I'm going steady with him.

Jane: Why not? You're always eying Charlie.

Mary: Well, so what! What do you think, Betty?

Jane: Betty agrees with me. Don't you, Betty?

Betty: Well, I don't think you should be fooling around with someone else's boyfriend, Jane. I wouldn't invite you to go along with me on a double date. No way!
(and on and on)

When *Courtroom* is played at a higher level of intensity, as in the case of a divorce, misdemeanor, or felony, the play takes place in an actual courtroom.

the wooden leg game   When people play *Wooden Leg*, they use some real or imaginary handicap as an excuse for not achieving anything. For example, one student was asked by a counselor why he didn't study harder and put more effort into learning how to read better. In his frustration, he responded, "What do you expect of me, I came from a broken home." This student had been using an unhappy family experience from his past as an excuse for not having to study or achieve anything significant. This kind of excuse is like pretending to have a major physical handicap. It's like saying, "What can you expect of a poor person with a wooden leg?" Rather than going ahead and doing whatever is possible, a person playing this game uses a handicap — social, physical, educational, personal background — in order to manipulate others and to belittle their achievement. People with serious handicaps may or may not play this game. Helen Keller, for example, didn't.

poor me games   Many games played from the Victim position come under the heading of *Poor Me*. People play this game when they indulge in feeling sorry for themselves and pitying themselves. They have taken the position that they are not-OK, they are not able to solve problems or learn how to do things in a new way. They get negative strokes out of complaining and whining and feeling sorry for themselves. "Why can't I be as good looking as the others (Poor Me)." "I never get the car (Poor Me)." "Everybody else stays out later. Why can't I? (Poor Me)." "Nobody else has to work on Saturday except me (Poor Me)."

A variation of *Poor Me* is *Ain't It Awful*. In this game the player does a lot of talking about how bad things are and often exclaims, "Ain't It Awful," and tries to get others to agree. Again, however, the player does not take any action to improve the situation. In fact, *Ain't It Awful* players keep things bad because it helps them perpetuate their role of phoney Rescuer.

Another variation of *Poor Me* is *Why Does This Always Happen To Me?* People who play this game tend to feel that they are singled out for bad things to happen to them. They suffer more misfortunes than other people. They may not be aware that unknowingly they arrange things or set things up so that something goes wrong.

Games that are played to get a put-down are often started by Victims. The players may take a physical stance or posture that makes them appear victimized. They may even use a tone of voice that is whiney, confused, or sad, which is part of the drama of playing the game. Usually Victims act like martyrs. In this self-sacrificing role they may appear as Persecutors to others. For example, a person who says accusingly, "I've given you so much, and I've sacrificed so much for you, I don't understand how you can talk to me that way," is playing the dialogue from the Victim role; however, the person being spoken to may feel persecuted by the *Poor Me* player.

Games people play to get themselves put down come out of negative childhood experiences. These experiences lead to decisions, such as "I can never please anyone," or "I'm stupid," or "I won't get close to people. They might die." These decisions are then crystallized into psychological positions and later reinforced with particular games. Games played from the Victim role reinforce some feeling of I'm not-OK, therefore I deserve to be put down.

**getting put-downs in
close relationships**

Sometimes people are attracted to one another because one wants to be put down and the other likes to do it. This kind of relationship reinforces their positions. Without knowing it, such people seem to be drawn to each other even though their relationship is often painful. As Penny expressed: "I don't know why I keep dating Scott. We fight all the time, and he's always criticizing how I talk and dress and everything. I feel like kicking myself, but I just can't seem to break off with him." Scott had a false sense of superiority, while Penny had a false sense of inferiority. Their relationship could be diagrammed like this:

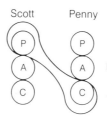

I'm OK because I know more than you and you're not-OK (so it's OK for me to kick you.)

I'm not-OK because I don't talk and dress right and you're OK (so it's OK to kick me.)

Such a relationship can be described as symbiotic. Each person is dependent upon the other to play a certain role and to operate from a certain ego state. Sooner or later many people get tired of this transactional pattern, and break off or become bored with each other. Relationships like this stifle the growth and development of each person, and people who play games to get themselves put down often get stuck in this kind of relationship.

exercises

1 evaluating case studies (group or individual)

Reread the case studies at the beginning of the unit (p. 119) and answer the following questions:

☐ What role did George seem to be playing?

☐ What kinds of things did George do to get his poor grades?

☐ What are the clues that George's behavior may be dishonest?

☐ What games was George likely to play?

☐ What role was Rosa playing?

☐ How would other people around Rosa feel?

☐ What games might Rosa play?

☐ What could have happened to Rosa to cause her to feel and act this way?

☐ How might people feel if they were to be around Howard a lot?

☐ What game was Howard playing and how seriously was he playing?

☐ If Howard doesn't change, how do you think his life might develop?

☐ What did Sarah and Alice each do to get a put-down?

☐ What games might they play with each other and with their boy friends?

2 games played to collect put-downs (group)

Review the games mentioned in this unit.

☐ Discuss how they might be acted out in school.

☐ Discuss how they might be acted out in families.

3 role-playing Victim games

Develop a skit which illustrates how a game with a Victim might be acted out in school or at home.

□ Each group presents their skit.

□ The rest of the class guesses which game is being acted out.

suggested research

1 the development of Victim games

Describe five different childhood experiences that might cause people to play games to get themselves put down.

□ What particular game would they choose to play?

□ How would they play it when they're children?

□ When they're in high school?

□ When they're adults?

2 winning in spite of handicaps

Many people do not use their handicaps to manipulate other people into games.

□ Describe someone you know well or a prominent person who has had serious misfortunes but has become a winner in spite of it.

20 games played to put others down

case study 1 Edith never seemed really to enjoy anything. No matter what she saw, or what she heard, she found some fault with it. She often said things such as, "I think Mr. Jones would be a good teacher if he didn't laugh so much." "The play was really great, but they needed a little more lighting on the left side of the stage." "Well, I'd go out with him but I hate the way he chews gum." "Oh, look at how that girl's dressed. The colors don't match." Some of her friends had tagged Edith a nitpicker.

case study 2 Darwin was the silent type. He seldom complained and usually went along with other people's decisions, although feeling resentful inside. When Darwin was alone, however, he would often review the events of the day in his head as though to "keep score" on others. When he felt he had taken things long enough, he would say to himself, "Just you wait. The next time anyone does that again I'll put him in his place." That was Darwin's pattern, to collect grievances and then feel justified in jumping on someone hard when a mistake was made.

case study 3 Roger was always trying to be helpful to other people. Even when he didn't know much about their problems, he would give them advice and tell them what he thought they should do. He often became annoyed with people who would question him with, "How come you know so much?" Sometimes if Roger's advice and ideas didn't work, a friend would come back and complain to him about it. When this happened, Roger would look dumbfounded, saying, "Well, I was just trying to help you out."

introduction to games that put others down Have you ever been around people who constantly pick out the little flaws in others? Or those who seem to be continually critical? Or noticed those who frequently put other people down when they catch them in the act of making a mistake?

Have you ever known anyone who is always giving advice, helping out, and trying to rescue others? If so, you have seen people acting out the basic Persecutor and Rescuer roles which are always present when a game is played to put somebody else down.

Persecutors use put-down games by being critical or punitive toward others. Rescuers use put-down games by treating others as if they were inadequate or helpless. People whose favorite role is that of a Persecutor or Rescuer often feel guilty, confused, or inadequate when in the Child ego state although they may not be aware of their basic feeling of being a Victim. Because they may hurt so much inside, they use one of the other two game roles in an effort to avoid their own pain or cover up their inner feelings of self-destruction.

There are many ways to catch other people making mistakes and to put them down. Three games that do it well are *Blemish, Now I've Got You,* and *Uproar.*

blemish   People who initiate the game of *Blemish* pick at the little faults in other people. They look for minor blemishes in the effort to prove that someone else is not-OK. For example, a teacher who plays *Blemish* with a book report may miss the creativeness of the report but catch the little mistakes and comment, "The report is all right, but you need to improve your spelling." If you have ever received a report back with all the mistakes pointed out and no comments about what was good, you have experienced what it feels like to have *Blemish* played with you.

As another example, a student who initiates *Blemish* may suddenly turn to a friend saying something like "You really look great in that color. Now, all you need is a haircut" or, "That shirt is stylish but doesn't fit your personality" or, "I wanted pizza but why the anchovies?" or, "You were five minutes late and now I don't feel like going." At home this same student might say, "Dinner was OK but the biscuits were too brown." or, "You've got four kinds of soda pop but none is the kind I like!"

People who play *Blemish* often feel blemished inside and not-OK. But rather than using their Adult to make their Child feel OK, they search for little flaws in other people in a futile attempt to relieve the pressure of their own not-OK feelings.

Like monkeys in a zoo they nit-pick each other. But unlike monkeys who nit-pick to help other monkeys, people do it for the purpose of putting others down or putting them off in the fear of being put-down themselves.

now i've got you   People who play the game of *Now I've Got You* wait for someone else to make a mistake and then strike out at them like a cobra, releasing venom and making the other person suffer. For example, one employer who played a mild form of this game often gave incomplete or unclear instructions. When the employee didn't do the work right, this employer would find fault with it and strike out by being critical in front of others. When playing a harder game, this same person threatened firing the worker and sometimes did. This felt like poison to the employees and spoiled their references.

Employees may also relish playing the games of *Now I've Got You* with the boss. It can give them a lot of satisfaction to find that the so-called authority figure makes mistakes too. It can give them a lot of satisfaction to find that the so-called authority figure makes mistakes too.

The same game can be played with friends or schoolmates. One person leaves money, jewelry, clothes, homework, or sports equipment around and then "catches" another person in the act of "borrowing" something without asking. The *Now I've Got You* player can thus accuse the other of stealing.

You can see how one person's *Kick Me* game and another's *Now I've Got You* may be complementary. One person provokes a criticism, hoping to get the familiar negative stroke for the Child; the other obliges by coming on as Critical Parent.

uproar   *Uproar* is often a loud game involving put-downs by each person. In *Uproar* people argue with each other. The game starts when one person's accusation or criticism hooks another's not-OK Child, which becomes defensive. The interchange quickly leads to feelings of resentment. When the right amount of resentment is collected the two players feel justified in turning their backs on each other and stamping away. Uproar usually leads to psychological or physical withdrawal.

1. Friend: "You were supposed to return my book today. I should have never given it to you. Now I'll be late with my assignment."

2. Friend: "Why didn't you tell me that. You said the end of the week, and today's only Wednesday."

1. Friend: "You know I have a math test Thursday. I'd have to have it on Wednesday in order to bone up for my test."

2. Friend: "You should have said so. You loaned me the book and told me not to worry about it till the end of the week.

1. Friend: "This always happens when I loan you something. It'll be your fault if I flunk my test."

2. Friend: "You've flunked plenty of tests without that excuse."

Uproar is now well on its way with accusations and defensiveness or counter-accusations between the two friends.

Uproar is also a common family game which isolates family members from each other and builds up resentment for the next game of *Uproar*.

Rescuers' put-down games   People who play *I'm Only Trying To Help You* usually operate from the manipulative Rescuer role. Such players may rescue people who don't need it or who don't want it. They may foul people up with well-meaning but poor advice in the guise of being helpful. When the rescue does not work, the Rescuer may look wide-eyed and astonished, saying "Why, I was only trying to help you."

In both *I'm Only Trying to Help You* and another game called *Why Don't You*, the Rescuer's function is one of showing how to do something or in giving advice. However, the techniques of the games and the payoffs are different. In *I'm Only*

Trying to Help You, the seemingly helpless person initially *accepts* the advice, then becomes a Persecutor, and strikes back when it doesn't work.

In *Why Don't You*, which is frequently the complementary game to *Yes, But* (discussed in Unit 18), the seemingly helpless player does *not* accept the Rescuer's advice, but, instead, refuses every suggestion because of the childhood decision that since nobody knew the answers then (when the child really needed them) nobody's going to give him answers now. The *Why Don't You* Rescuer is ground down and ends up feeling the frustration and confusion characteristic of a Victim.

Rescuers rarely help anybody. In fact, they often make others feel dependent upon them so that they can have a Victim to save and thus feel temporarily OK.

People who play games as Persecutors also tend to seek out people who play games as Victims. This combination insures an ongoing game and negative strokes as the payoff.

summary   In summary, people act in many ways and play many games to put others down. They can do this from either persecuting or rescuing positions. Persecutors do it with games such as *Blemish, Now I've Got You,* and *Uproar.* Rescuers do it by being over-solicitous or over-protective with games such as *I'm Only Trying to Help You* and *Why Don't You.* Both Persecutors and Rescuers give off the message to others: "You're Not-OK."

exercises

NOW THAT MOM'S GONE, IT'S UP TO ME

1 evaluating case studies (group or individual)

Reread the case studies at the beginning of the unit (page 125) and answer the following questions:

□ What role did Edith play a lot of the time?

□ How would Edith's game affect her friendships?

□ How might Darwin's game affect his friendships?

□ What role was Roger playing in the case study?

□ How might Roger's games affect his friendships?

2 games to give put-downs (group)

Review the games mentioned in this unit and discuss how they might be acted out in school or at home.

3 role-playing Persecutor and Rescuer games (group)

Develop a skit which illustrates how a Rescuer and Persecutor game might be acted out in school or at home or on the job.

□ Each group presents their skit.

□ The rest of the class guesses which game is being acted out.

suggested research

1 the development of persecutor games

Describe three different childhood experiences that might cause people to play games to persecute others.

□ What particular game might they choose to play?

□ How would they have played it when they were children?

□ When they are in high school?

□ When they are older?

2 the development of rescuer games

Describe three different childhood experiences that might cause people to play games to rescue others.

□ What particular game might they choose to play?

□ How would they have played it when they were children?

□ When they are in high school?

□ When they are older?

21 identifying games

case study 1 Laurie's chores included feeding her dog. For over a year every evening around 7:00 p.m. the same thing happened between Laurie and her mother. Laurie would be studying and would "not remember" her dog. Her mother would start reminding her in a calm and pleasant voice. Eventually, however, her voice would become more tense. Next she would become angry and shout, "We bought that dog for you, and you promised to take care of it. You'd let the poor thing starve to death if I didn't keep after you. You either take care of that dog or I'm going to get rid of it!"

case study 2 Todd and Patrice spent hours on the phone but often after Patrice hung up she would feel disappointed. "Sometimes", she said to her sister, "I think Todd is just plain stupid. He always says he doesn't understand or that he feels confused. When I explain something all over again, he still doesn't catch on. When he's hurt or sick and says so, that's OK. It's just when he acts confused and I don't seem to be able to do anything about it that I feel awful. I don't know why I think I have to get him unconfused."

case study 3 Viola was shy, "a shrinking violet", her mother often called her. However, if things got tough for someone else, Viola would jump into the situation and try to rescue the victim like a mother bear protecting her cubs. Everyone where she worked knew that Viola could be counted on to come to the rescue. If someone was being put down by someone else, Viola would try to intervene and smooth things over.

case study 4 When Rick went home from his TA class, his mother had a letter in her hand and was looking despondent. Without asking what the letter said, Rick accused her, "There, you are feeling sorry for yourself playing the role of Victim." His mother looked up sobbing, "But, Ricky, this letter says Uncle Dave just died. And you know how close we were."

the intensity of games   All people play psychological games. Some play "soft" games that leave them or others with a mild negative feeling. These are called first-degree games.

Some people play "hard" games in which they are "going for broke." These games may end with suicide or homicide and are called third-degree games.

Others play games that are somewhere between the two extremes. These games are called second-degree games. The players often end up by doing some kind of quitting — dropping out school, leaving home, breaking off an important relationship.

People are seldom aware that they play games. Usually it is not until the series of transactions are finished, leaving someone feeling not-OK, that a person may become aware that something was going on which was not quite on the level.

Games often start when one person, wearing a psychological sweatshirt with a message, attracts another person whose sweatshirt hints at a complementary role. For example, a person who wears a "Poor-Me" shirt is likely to pick out one who wears a "Don't-worry-I'll-rescue-you" shirt, or a "Watch-out-I'll-persecute-you" shirt.

Games are sometimes easy to spot because of the obvious put-downs. However, there are other ways to identify them. Here are four ways that may give you some additional clues. (They are discussed in the following pages.)

1. drawing a transactional diagram showing the ulterior transactions

2. identifying game roles and the switch in the roles

3. using the game formula

4. discovering the basic game plan

the transactional game   The use of the *transactional diagram* to analyze games consists of drawing (1) each
diagram   person's ego states (2) figuring out the plausible (overt) surface transaction which appears Adult to Adult and (3) the ulterior (covert) transactions going on between them.

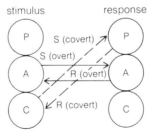

a transactional game diagram

The above diagram could represent the game of *Schlemiel*. The player breaks something, spills ink on the new rug at his friends's house, cracks up the car, and then appears so remorseful that others are invited to forgive him. For example, Les was known for being a "butterfingers" and one of his typical transactions was:

Les: (Breaks mimeograph machine)

Teacher: Oh, no. That's our newest machine. We've only had it for a week!

Les: How could I have done such a clumsy thing. I'm always doing some fool thing like this. I'm so clumsy. Gee, I'm sorry.

Teacher: Now don't feel bad, Les. We'll get it fixed some way. You go to class and I'll get this mess cleaned up.

Les's ulterior transaction throughout his game is "Love me no matter what I do." The teacher first feels like persecuting him, but then is hooked by Les's apologetic stance, and switches into the Nurturing Parent to rescue him.

the game roles   When people play games they unknowingly start in one role and often switch to another. For example, a person may come on as a Rescuer playing *I'm Only Trying to Help You* and then switch to Victim when the help is refused or criticized. Or, a parent may bawl out a child — coming on Persecutor and maybe playing *Uproar* — then later have guilty feelings like a Victim. Or a student may start off in a Victim position and then turn Persecutor, rejecting another person's help. The game roles of Victim, Persecutor, and Rescuer can be diagramed on a triangle. [8] The arrows indicate the way roles may be switched.

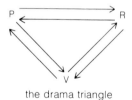

the drama triangle

The roles are diagramed this way because people who feel like Victims often need others to act as Persecutors to punish them or act as Rescuers to "save" them. People in the role of Victims are frequently in the I'm not-OK, You're OK position: I'm not-OK and deserve to be rescued or persecuted; You're OK and have the power to rescue or persecute me.

Many people who think of themselves as Victims have punitive Parents and/or rescuing Parents in their heads. Such people may wear different sweatshirts when they are in different ego states. For example, one person may wear an "I'm helpless" sweatshirt and play *Poor Me* games when in the Child ego state, and then switch inwardly to Parent. In the Parent ego state, this same person might wear a different sweatshirt, "I'm the big boss," and play a different game, *Now I've Got You* (as a parent figure did) or they may play *I'm Only Trying to Help You*, switching to another parent figure whose sweatshirt was "Just call me any time for help." This could be diagramed:

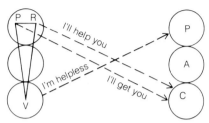

sweatshirts and ego states

the game formula   The use of the *game formula* is another way to identify games. It clearly shows how the game starts, how the second player is "hooked" into responding, how the switch of roles is accomplished, and how each person ends up with a psychological trading stamp. The game formula is as follows:

$$C + G = R \rightarrow S \rightarrow X \rightarrow P$$

C = the con, the ulterior message player 1 sends to player 2.

G = the gimmick, a weak spot in player 2, such as self-righteousness, sentimentality, criticalness, and cruelty.

R = the response that player 2 makes if hooked.

S = the switch, which is an unexpected next move by player 1.

X = the cross-up, which is player 2 being thrown off balance because of the unexpected switch.

P = the payoff that each player receives (old feelings, trading stamps)

Dr. Eric Berne tells of a patient who asked for reassurance, received it, and then put it down. The game went like this:

'Do you think I'll get better, doctor? [the con]. The sentimental therapist [the weak spot, the gimmick] replied 'Of course you will'. At that point the patient revealed her ulterior motive in asking the question. Instead of saying 'Thank you,' as in a straight transaction, she pulled the switch [the role switch] with: "What makes you think you know everything?"[9]

The doctor was thrown off balance by this response (the cross-up). And they both collected feelings (the payoff). The therapist was frustrated and the patient was elated.

The process of this formula can also be more briefly outlined as:

Player 1 does something that attracts (hooks) player 2.

Player 2 is hooked, because of her or his weak spot.

Player 2 responds.

Player 1 pulls a switch by doing something unexpected.

Player 2 feels confused.

Both 1 and 2 collect a psychological trading stamp.

A familiar situation that occurs in families goes like this:

Mother	(with concern):	"What grade did you get in your algebra exam?"
Son	(dejectedly):	"I got a D (with sarcasm). What did you expect!"
Mother	(defensively):	"What do you mean, what did I expect!"
Son	(angrily):	"You know darn well. You sent me to a dozen stores and I didn't have time to study. If it weren't for you I could have had an A."
Mother	(cuttingly):	"That'll be the day."

They both collect bad feelings as the game ends.

If player 1 is aware of games and decides not to play them, the games won't start. If player 2 is aware of her or his weak spots that could be hooked and decides not to play games, the games won't continue.

the game plan   Each game has a plan of action and a final play. The name of the game is not as important as learning how to spot the plan and identify the plays that occur over and over. The game plan focuses on predictable patterns and payoffs. To use the game plan ask the following questions and write down the answers:

What keeps happening over and over that leaves someone feeling bad?

How does it start?

What happens next?

How does it end?

How does each person feel when it ends?

Following is an example of the game plan regularly played by a father and daughter:

Sis:	(Asks a favor.)
Pa:	No.
Sis:	Why not?
Pa:	Because, last time you . . . (put down) . . .
Sis:	Well, that's not true . . .

Pa and Sis:	(Argue loudly).
Sis:	(Leaves the room, yelling.)
Pa:	(Reads the paper.)
Pa:	(Feels mad.)
Sis:	(Feels mad.)

When first aware of this game plan, both Pa and Sis thought the other person ought to stop doing this or that. Eventually, they made a mutually acceptable contract regarding the granting of favors. They also contracted that neither person would put the other down and that neither would yell. Thus, they contracted to respond differently at several steps in the game.[10]

There are several advantages to analyzing games by using the game plan:

1. By breaking down the games into moves, each player's Adult is hooked in analyzing and evaluating.

2. The game plan personalizes or individualizes each person's unique game pattern and is, therefore, recognized as more relevent.

3. It is not necessary to know all the games by name. In fact, other more ingenious names can be devised by people for their particular plan.

4. It can be used to analyze childhood games as well as those played in later life, at home, at school, and at work.

the game of psychiatry   Everybody can use the new psychological tools of TA to understand themselves better, improve their lives, and gain more insight into the actions and attitudes of others. Some people, however, misuse the concepts and language of TA. They over- analyze and this puts others down. This is the destructive game of *Psychiatry*. A person who plays this game might say, "You come on Parent and make me feel like a Child." Thus she or he takes no responsibility for personal feelings and lays the blame for bad feelings at the feet of friends, family, and acquaintances. A person playing *Psychiatry* might make other accusations such as:

"You're playing games with me."

"I'm sick of you acting the Victim role."

"I'd be fine if you weren't playing the Persecutor all the time."

"All you do is cross-transact with me."

summary   In summary, all people play games and play them at different levels of intensity. Games can be identified in four ways: the transactional diagram, the game roles, the game formula, and the game plan. To accuse others of playing games is not an effective way to break them up. Discovering one's own games and giving them up in favor of authentic, open, and honest transactions is effective and a sign of a winner.

exercises

1 evaluating case studies (group or individual)

Review the case studies at the beginning of the unit (page 130) and answer the following questions:

☐ What was Laurie's game with her mother?

☐ What games were Todd and Patrice likely to play?

☐ What was Viola's game plan?

☐ What destructive game did Rick play with his mother?

2 identifying games (group)

Divide the class into four groups. Each group takes one of the methods of identifying games (see page 131.)

☐ Select two games to identify using the method your group is assigned.

☐ The each group demonstrates how they identified these games to the remainder of the class.

☐ Which group gets the most strokes for creativity?

3 identifying roles (group)

Post several large sheets of paper on the wall.

☐ Label each sheet as Victim, Persecutor, or Rescuer.

☐ Write adjectives on each of the sheets to describe each of the game roles.

☐ Write phrases that people in each of the roles might use.

☐ Add brief body-language descriptions for each role.

suggested research

1 your game roles

Think back over some of the transactions that you've had in the last week.

☐ Did you feel like a Victim, Persecutor, or Rescuer?

☐ If you felt like a Victim, did you provoke anyone to treat you that way?

☐ If you felt like a Persecutor, did you put anybody else down?

☐ If you felt like a Rescuer, did you try to rescue someone who didn't really want it?

☐ How do you think you learned to play your games?

22 breaking up games

case study 1 Ms. Brewster became concerned over the amount of time she spent after school with Kathy, giving her personal help and counseling. She began to realize that Kathy came to her over and over again acting helpless and confused — not understanding the assignments, having problems with her friends and family, and expressing fears of not being able to graduate. However, every time Ms. Brewster offered Kathy advice or counsel, Kathy found some reason to either explain that it wouldn't work, that she had already tried it, or that it was just too hard for her to do. After each encounter Ms. Brewster felt frustrated because Kathy didn't accept any help yet sought it over and over. Finally Ms. Brewster figured out that perhaps she should quit trying to be so helpful to Kathy and give Kathy more of the responsibility for solving her own problems. The next time Kathy came in for advice Ms. Brewster didn't give it to her. Instead she simply said, "That is a tough problem, Kathy. What are you doing about it?" She then heard Kathy out, but continued to pass the problem back to her instead of jumping in to solve it. This happened several times but eventually Kathy's visits became less frequent.

case study 2 Matt always felt he got the short end of the stick both in his family and in his friendships at school. He felt picked on and put down and often spent long hours pouting about how "Nobody likes me." In a TA class, Matt discovered that he initiated put-down transactions by wearing a Victim sweatshirt. He also figured out how he was verbally apologetic about himself and how he invited other people to treat him like a Victim. Matt made the decision to use his Adult to stop playing this role. When he first tried to change, he found that he often slipped back into the Victim role. But gradually his confidence in himself grew and he stopped provoking others to find fault with him. One of Matt's closest friends confided in him "I don't know what's happened, Matt, but you've become much more sure of yourself, and you are easier to be around."

case study 3 Lenny was avoided by all of the students in his class because when he became angry it was with a roar. Furthermore, Lenny was so tall, heavy, and strong that his anger was frightening. During his junior year he wanted to go out for wrestling but was turned down by the coach who told him, "You'll have to prove you can control yourself before I'll have you on the team." Lenny was so eager to be on the team that he decided to change his behavior. This was not easy. He had intimidated others for so long that his habit was a tough one to break. But he did it.

case study 4   Ms. Juarez, the math teacher at City High, was solid in appearance, manner, and behavior. She was also pleasant to be with. Often, students who had difficulty with their math or personal lives would seek her out between classes, after school, or even on the parking lot. When episodes occurred in the hall or class room that might throw other teachers into a rage, Ms. Juarez remained unruffled. She would discuss the situation, in a calm voice, take appropriate action, then continue on with the day's assignments.

using the Adult to   If you want to stop playing games, the first step is to understand clearly the theory of
break up games   what games are, the moves, and the payoffs. The second step is to recognize your own favorite game role. Next you can discover how the game roles of others complement yours, what you do to each other as you move through a game, and why it usually ends up with bad feelings.

When people become aware of games, they can take intelligent steps to stop them. They can stop initiating the play, and they can avoid being "hooked" into playing. Information about the games people play should not be used to control others and to "cure" them of their bad habits. When it is, it's a game in itself.

The Adult ego state is needed to break up games. The Adult can figure out what would be more appropriate to do instead of continuing the game. In other words, the Adult is needed to determine what other options are available. With enough practice, new behavior patterns can be tried out, developed, and repeated again and again until they take the place of the old ones. As with everything, the more you do it, the easier it gets.

Although some people play "skull" games and kick themselves inside their own heads, games are generally a two-person transaction. Consequently, either person in a transaction can break up a game.

stop playing the   Since games are two-way transactions, one way to stop playing someone else's
complementary hand   game is to avoid playing the complementary hand. For example, if a person has a friend who plays *Yes, But*, the complementary hand is to give advice and helpful suggestions. The game is thwarted if such advice is not given, and instead, the problem is reflected back to the person who laid it out. Or give a simple answer such as, "I really don't know the best thing you could do about that." This is often an easy way to stop the game. Then a crossed transaction, as was discussed in Unit 13, will occur. Stopping games is a positive use of crossed transactions.

138

stop playing Victim, Persecutor, or Rescuer

Games always involve the manipulative roles of Victim, Persecutor, and Rescuer. One way for people to stop their own games is to stop playing any of these roles. Stop thinking of yourself as a Victim, acting helpless and dependent, when you are really able to stand alone. Stop seeing yourself as a Persecutor, criticizing those who don't need it. Stop reinforcing your image as a Rescuer, helping those who don't need help, or helping when you resent it after all.

When people stop playing manipulative roles, it often involves a change even in their body language. For example, a person in the Victim role frequently takes on a body stance that has all the stage directions for playing a helpless, hurt, or dependent person. She or he may look anxious, downcast, and stoop-shouldered. When Victim games stop, a person shows confidence in posture and tone of voice.

stop exaggerating

People who play games tend to exaggerate. They exaggerate their own weaknesses and strengths and often exaggerate the weaknesses and strengths of others. One way to help stop playing games is to stop this kind of exaggeration. For example, people who are continually apologizing for themselves, saying such things as, "I could kick myself for having done that" or "How stupid of me" can become aware that this is a put-down of themselves and can learn to stop exaggerating their own shortcomings.

stop misusing time

Some people are always playing games, others play them less frequently. But whatever the level of intensity and the frequency with which they are played, games take up lots of time. If people choose to give up their games, they will be able to do better things with their time. For example, they might learn new skills, exercise their talents, find a new friend, try out a new hobby, or spend more time enjoying themselves. Time can be structured in ways that are positively related to the here and now rather than to reinforcing negative childhood feelings.

stop collecting negative strokes

As people stop game playing they may feel deprived at first. Something that seemed essential to their life is gone. That "something" is likely to be the negative stroke. People *need* strokes. When they give up games, they give up giving and getting the negative strokes that are the game payoffs. Instead, they give and get positive strokes. While negative strokes are better than none, positive strokes are the best of all. So a former game player learns how to get more positive strokes.

In the beginning this must be planned and deliberate. One certain way to get positive strokes is to be more generous in giving them. People who learn to stroke others in a constructive way and do this frequently attract the same kinds of strokes from other people. Positive interchanges of strokes helps create longer lasting friendships. To *have* friends, a person must learn how to *be* a friend.

139

exercises

1 evaluating case studies (group or individual)

Reread the case studies at the beginning of the unit (pp. 137-138) and answer the following questions:

☐ What game did Ms. Brewster seem to be playing with Kathy?

☐ What game did Kathy seem to be playing with her teacher?

☐ How did Ms. Brewster successfully break up this game? Why did it work?

☐ What kind of game was Matt playing?

☐ What seemed to be his primary role?

☐ What did Matt do to break up his game?

☐ How did this affect Matt's friendships?

☐ What was Lenny's favorite role and game?

☐ What did he need to do to change his pattern?

☐ Do you think Ms. Juarez was playing games? If so, why? If not, why not?

2 role-playing stopping games (individual or group)

Select three games in which the transactions are clear to the people in your group. Write out how each of the games starts.

☐ What happens next?

☐ How does each game conclude?

Now develop a strategy for stopping each game.

Select one or two of the games to role play for the entire class. First role play the whole

game. Have the class guess which game was played. Next do an "instant replay" and break up the game.

3 identifying games and roles (individual)

Read through the following dialogue. Identify the roles of Victim, Rescuer, or Persecutor being acted out by each person.

Son: (yells angrily)	"You know I hate blue. Here you went and bought me another blue shirt!"
Mother:	"I never do anything right as far as you're concerned."
Father:	"Don't you dare yell at your mother like that, young man. Go to your room and no dinner!"
Son: (sulking in his room)	They tell me to be honest, and when I tell them what I don't like, they put me down. How can you satisfy people like that?"
Mother: (sneaks him a tray of food)	"Now don't tell your father. We shouldn't get so upset over a shirt."
Mother: (returns to father)	"John, you're so tough with our son. I'll bet he's sitting in his room right now hating you."
Father:	"Gee, honey, I was only trying to help you, and you kick me where it hurts the most."
Son: (calling out)	"Hey Mom, lay off, will ya? Dad's just tired."

What three games are being played?

What makes you think so?

_____   _____

_____   _____

_____   _____

suggested research

1 breaking up your games

Figure out one or two games you think you might be playing.

□ What is the first transaction in this game? In other words, how do you get it started?

□ What role do you play?

□ What role do you switch to?

□ Develop a strategy for not making the first move.

□ What are three things that you might do as alternatives to starting this game?

You may want to make these notes in your personal journal.

23 cultural and subcultural scripts

case study 1   Manuel lived in a Mexican-American community. At fifteen he showed signs of a developing beard and began to grow a mustache. His family was very proud of his new look. However, the school officials soon asked him to shave and chided him for taking pride in what they called his messy appearance. At home, his mother exclaimed, "But that's the sign of Spanish blood. What's the matter with your teachers?" Manuel felt caught between wanting to please his family and himself and wanting to please the school. He complained to a friend, "Wow, if we Chicanos speak Spanish at school, we really get it in the neck. At home, if I speak anything but Spanish, my father blows his stack. Now I've got another problem. My teacher says I have to shave off my mustache. My mom says it's great and shows I'm a real man. How can a guy win!"

case study 2   Judy was of Japanese descent. She was very courteous and never interrupted when someone else was speaking. At home she deferred to her parents at all times; at school she maintained an air of deference and obedience. When asked by a casual acquaintance why she was so quiet and why she only went around with other people of Japanese descent, Judy replied, "I just can't imagine being any other way and my friends like the same things as I do."

case study 3   Zachary's father was out of work and moved from the country to the city to try to find a job. For the first time, Zachary was going to a large city school instead of a small rural one. His first day was miserable. He didn't know anyone, his clothes weren't hip, and he didn't understand the "in" language. Zachary felt completely isolated from the other people at the school. Late at night after his parents were long asleep he would toss and turn in his bed. "Why is everyone so different in this school?" he would agonize. "What's the matter with me anyhow?"

case study 4   Suzanne's ancestors were of pioneering stock. Each in their own way had pioneered new ideas and new ways of doing things. Suzanne's father did early research in dental hygiene. Her mother was a professional artist at a time when most artists were men. Two of her grandparents were early pioneers in Alaska during the gold-rush days. Her great-grandmother was a teacher and a pioneer of new scientific theories. Suzanne was happiest when thinking about a new idea or pioneering a new school project.

introduction to cultural scripts

Have you ever noticed how people carry on cultural traditions generation after generation? How they express the same values and similar ways of doing things as their forefathers? How, when they move to a new country, for example, they often bring with them traditions about all kinds of things, even ways of eating? For example, some sit on the floor, some on chairs. Some eat with chopsticks, some hold their knives and forks one way, while others use them another way.

These customs become part of a *cultural script* and are expressed in words such as, "That's the way *we* do things." Cultural scripts are the accepted and expected dramatic patterns that occur within a society. They are determined by the spoken and unspoken assumptions about people and events that are believed by the majority of people within that group. Cultural scripts prescribe the traditional ways of doing things.

Like theatrical scripts, cultural scripts have themes, characters, expected roles, stage directions, costumes, settings, scenes, and final curtains. Cultural scripts reflect what is thought of as the national character.

Scripts differ from one culture to another. For example, some cultural scripts contain themes of persecution and abuse. Such a theme has been part of the ancient Jewish script since the beginning of the history of the Jews. Black slaves brought from Africa had a similar script imposed upon them; so had women, to a lesser degree. In recent times these groups have started rewriting their scripts.

Some cultural scripts are quite different. Their characters, rather than being victimized themselves, *make others suffer*. For example, building empires by making conquests was part of the ancient Romans' script which imposed suffering on others. Currently, nations that exploit the "third world" are acting out similar patterns. Still other nations *act as rescuers,* stepping in to "save" the oppressed and impoverished.

Throughout history, nations and their peoples have acted from persecutor positions as conquerors or rescuer positions as saviors, or victim positions as the conquered ones. Sometimes their rescue and victim positions are legitimate, sometimes not.

pioneer and settler cultural scripts

When the USA was forming, many people came as victims, leaving their homeland to escape political and religious oppression. Others came as persecutors intending to exploit the land and its people. A few saw themselves as rescuers, saving the land from "less desirable" conquerors.

All of these groups experienced a basic theme: the struggle for survival. In many cases, this struggle was acted out by settlers building towns, establishing schools, and putting down roots. History shows that both pioneers and settlers were victims, persecutors, and rescuers — sometimes legitimately so, sometimes not. When hard games were played people ended up massacred or swinging from trees.

Early pioneers were always on the move, taking risks, and exploring the country for the settlers who were to follow. Even though some of the scenery, acts, characters, and action changed, the basic theme often remained the same — looking for new challenges. Today a similar pioneering script is being acted out by the astronauts though with different costumes and settings. Coonskin caps have given way to complicated headgear, horses to spaceships, Grandma's Sunday pot roasts to food from plastic bags. The scenery has changed from lands and waters to space and moon dust; the action from self-reliance to technical dependency. Space pioneers, like their earlier counterparts, may be setting a new scene for settlers who will someday follow. Not all pioneering is geographical, however. The same spirit can be observed on scientific and social frontiers.

In contrast to the pioneers' script of always being on the move, the first American settlers' script was to dig in and put down roots. Settlers tilled the soil, built homes and towns, established businesses, worked hard to acquire material goods and to increase the population. Their struggle was hard, and their lives short and precarious.

new script themes   Currently a large segment of American society—certainly not all of it—is no longer preoccupied with the struggle for individual survival. Modern-day settlers have life expectancies approaching 80 years. Rather than working independently, they are likely to work for a large corporation or the government. Instead of struggling for bare physical survival, they may find themselves caught up in the pleasures and problems of affluence.

As times change new script themes emerge: getting educated, making money, seeking pleasure, and searching for life's meaning. Today we are again facing the "struggle for survival" theme as it reemerges in terms of survival of the human race, the preservation of the natural environment, and the dwindling supply of resources.

In addition to themes, cultural scripts usually dictate specific roles. For example, most cultures differentiate — rationally or irrationally — between the roles men play and those expected of women. Specific roles may also be expected from subcultures. For example, bellboys, pawnbrokers, gardeners, and so forth may come traditionally from certain racial or ethnic groups.

Culture is transmitted from Parent ego states to Parent ego states, generation after generation. People either submit to these traditions or they rebel against them or modify them. When they submit, the traditions are passed on to others. When they rebel, the traditions may be changed. Most of us see ourselves and the world from our own cultural points of view. In a multicultural society such as ours, there will be many points of view, each thought to be "right."

subcultural scripting   When a culture is large and complex, subcultures exist within it. Some of the words used to designate such subcultures are: *ethnic groups, racial groups,* and *national groups.* Subcultures are often defined by geographical location, religious beliefs, sex, education, age, or other common bonds. For example, in small, less complex cultures it was and is common for youths to imitate their elders, looking forward to being like them. However, today it is not uncommon for young people to set themselves apart from the authority figures by dress, hair styles, tastes in music, dance, vocabulary. In addition, they may place a high value on the opinions of their peer group and discount the opinions of the older generation.

Each subculture, whether defined by age or some other element, evolves it own dramatic actions. The persons within it may identify themselves by saying "we." And may identify other subcultures by saying "those."

We Texans	Those Easterners
We Presbyterians	Those Jews
We Blacks	Those Whities
We Chicanos	Those Gringos

It appears that human beings are frequently suspicious of differences. They often reflect such mistrust by taking a group position of We're OK but — (referring to those who are different—They are not-OK. This is contamination which becomes part of the accepted group thinking. If traditional thinking, which is generally passed on from Parent ego state to Parent ego state, goes unexamined by the Adult, strong feelings often rule rather than reason. As a result one group may be pitted against another group, each seeing itself as right. Consequently, conflict often erupts between subcultural scripts: rich versus poor, liberal versus conservative, uneducated versus educated.

Every culture and subculture has group prejudices which are believed in and acted out. These group prejudices are similar to ones held by individuals and are equally strong since they are constantly being reinforced by the group. People are not born with prejudice; they learn it. They learn which differences to fear, respect, or hate.

Derogatory terms often express the subcultural prejudices. People of one group may be patronizing to those of another, saying "Why, some of my best friends are . . ." Remarks like these may be well-intentioned but, for some, are hurtful.

Ethnic humor with stories of Pat and Mike, or Abie and Izzie, or Rastus and Mandy Lou also point to differences and to cultural stereotypes. Exaggerations of the speech and mannerisms of Negroes, Jews, Italians, and other groups are often mildly disguised but still derogatory. The exaggerations are not always unfavorable, yet many reflect discrimination in some form.

In addition to the use of labels and mannerisms which establish distance between cultures and subcultures, there are several other common patterns such as avoidance, restriction, and segregation.[11]

147

Avoidance is learned early in life when parents or playmates show children whom to associate with and whom to avoid. Later in life this learned avoidance may be acted out through economic boycotts and restrictive residential neighborhoods.

Clubs and private schools often *restrict* membership to a particular subculture and, although restrictive membership may be generally declining because of new civil rights laws, many of these restrictions are still approved of by large groups of people.

Segregation, which is based on trying to keep a certain category of people "in their place," is seldom voluntary except for a few notable exceptions such as the Amish people. The restriction of many American Indians to reservations, the past segregation of many Japanese-Americans to "security camps" following the attack on Pearl Harbor in 1941, and the segregation of blacks in ghettos are historical examples of involuntary segregation which involve physical deprivation, social distance, and ostracism. Extreme forms of subcultural prejudice may lead to tragic scenes of mob aggression and genocide.

A less obvious but no less tragic separation is inflicted on old people. More and more people are living into old age and many are not accepted as still productive members of society. It is becoming increasingly common for people in the over-sixty-five age group to be segregated and avoided. Their final years are frequently sad ones. This is particularly true of women. Two out of three of the elderly are women. Most live out their old age in poverty and loneliness.

The dramatic differences subcultures can introduce are allowable only in a tolerant larger culture. Yet, even in a tolerant culture many individuals will be fearful of differences. Each nation has its own unique script patterns concerning subcultures and whether or not they will be accepted, exploited, feared, or admired.

assimilation and pluralism

Two ways of dealing with cultural differences are assimilation and pluralism. *Assimilation* is the blending of groups. People from very different customs and backgrounds may try to blend in and become more like the people in the larger culture. For example, they may *change* their names, their customs, their style of dressing, even hair styles, so that they fit into the pattern of the established culture.

Pluralism, unlike assimilation, implies cultural variety rather than similarity. Although people from various cultures may be in contact with one another, they maintain their separate identities — their own scripts. This separatism is often expressed by people who *keep* their names, their customs and traditions, their style of dressing, and hair style. They do not change these things because they want to keep their identity rather than assimilate.

exercises

1 evaluating case studies (group or individual)

Reread the case studies at the beginning of the unit (pp. 144-145) and explore the following possibilities for each of them:

☐ Imagine what the grandparents were like. What would be some similarities and differences between their life style and the grandchild's?

2 subcultural patterns (group or individual)

Identify and discuss or write about examples of assimilation and pluralism in your community.

☐ Do you think one of these methods of relating to a larger culture is better than the other?

☐ Which method seems to work well in your community? Why?

3 the game plan and subcultural scripts (group or individual)

Often without being aware of it schools have subcultures that "play games" with other subcultures. Think of your school subcultures. Make a list of them (you may want to include cliques):

☐ Is there anything that keeps happening over and over again that leaves one group feeling not-OK?

☐ How does it start?

☐ How does it end?

If the situation is negative, what could be done to improve it?

suggested research

1 cultural interview

Interview an elderly person such as a grandparent or neighbor. Tell them you are studying various cultures and ask the person to discuss the following questions:

☐ Where did you live and what was it like when you were young?

☐ What cultural changes are most noticeable to you since that time?

☐ What changes do you think are for the better and what for the worse?

2 your genealogy

☐ Write up a brief summary of your genealogy. Do you have any famous or infamous ancestors?

☐ If you were adopted and do not know your biological inheritance, write up a genealogy of one of your adopted parents. If you prefer, invent your own genealogy.

24 family scripts and sexual identity

case study 1   Pat, a senior student in school, reported, "Our family script has its roots in Ireland. Every son has to be an altar boy. First Communion day is as important as a birthday. The oldest son is always expected to become a priest. At least one daughter is expected to enter the convent. In fact, I remember deciding against being a priest when I was about nine because I like to wear jeans and sweatshirts. My parents are still upset."

case study 2   Henrietta, when discussing her family script said, "In our family the boys follow in the footsteps of their father. They are expected to be farmers. The girls make their husbands and children their careers, and anything else is attacked for being unfeminine. Mother often said, 'The Lord made you female to have children and to take care of a husband. Running the world is for men.' It's always been this way in our family. So when I decided to become a veterinarian, it caused a lot of arguments. I had mixed feelings. Part of me felt proud of myself; another part felt as if I'd done something wrong and disgraced my family. What a bind to be caught in!"

case study 3   Bob was not what his parents wanted. After having had four boys, they definitely wanted a girl. At his birth they complained bitterly about "just another boy." Neighbors joshed about the future family basketball team, but the parents remained fixed in their negative feelings of Bob's being a boy. Even when he grew older they often lamented, "Why couldn't you have been a girl? We had the name Barbara all picked out."

case study 4   Charlene was exactly what her parents wanted — petite and charming. She was always the center of attention. When guests came over, Charlene was encouraged to do "cute things" for their approval. Her father often commented, "The way that little girl flirts is really something. She won't need much education. She'll get any man she goes after."

family scripts   When cultural and subcultural scripts are perpetuated, it is usually done through the family. Most families follow dramatic patterns which are similar to the cultural scripts. Some families develop what is their "family drama" and teach their children to play the appropriate roles in order to carry on this drama for many generations. Such dramas may be constructive, destructive, or go nowhere.

Family scripts often contain identifiable traditions and expectations for each family member. The script, in order to continue, must be successfully transmitted from generation to generation via the Parent ego state. Historically, such scripts are observable in certain prominent families that for generations have produced philanthropists, politicians, or professionals. Such scripts may also be present for generations among the poor and the uneducated. Losers run in families. So do winners.

When family scripts are perpetuated, family members might be adapted to believe that their particular family has a predetermined destiny. "We've never produced a skilled professional." "We Grahams have always lived off the land and always will." "We Lopez's will always be the life blood of this community." "We Kellys have been in politics for generations." "The traditions in our family would not allow us to be cowards." "In our family we'd starve rather than ask for help." "The Freedmans have always been a cut above others." "Everyone's down on us Joneses." "The women in our family have always been tough as crabgrass." "In our family, the home is a man's castle." "No one in our family has ever amounted to anything." "We Juks have never had a chance."

Some family scripts call for the offspring to follow certain lines of work. "There's always been a doctor in our family." "We Schmidts come from a long line of educators." "We Fabrizio women have always made good nurses." "We Bosmans have produced three generations of politicians." "There's always at least one failure in our family." "The sons in our family will uphold the traditions of the armed services." "It's in our blood to be leaders."

When a family member does not live up to the script expectation, he or she is often thought of as the "black sheep." However, a particular family script might call for a black sheep to add intrigue and interest to the family scene.

changing family scripts   Not all families perpetuate family scripts. In fact, many family members work deliberately to throw off the traditional scripts of the "old country" or those of the older generation. They prefer to be assimilated into the larger culture. Some traditions simply die because they are difficult to maintain when circumstances change rapidly. This can be experienced as "cultural shock." Cultural shock happens when the rate of change is so rapid that people have a hard time keeping up with it and adapting. Currently, because of rapid social and economic change, new scripts are evolving. There is less a feeling of belonging to a community. There is also a weakening of the tight family structure which leads to further changes.

For example, more people turn to the government for assistance rather than to their families as in previous generations. Furthermore, families are becoming smaller. Many couples decide not to have children or to have only one or two. Another trend is that grown children no longer take care of their aging parents. Often, children, parents, and grandparents are also separated by distance — either geographical, emotional, or intellectual — and have difficulty even spending holidays together. Some people are living together in groups or communes even though they are unrelated.

Many family scripts need changing. For example, families in the United States, poverty-stricken for generations, have low expectations for their family members. The children are scripted for failure generation after generation by society as well as by the family. It is difficult for uneducated people to compete on an equal footing with those who are better educated. The uneducated often become chronic losers. In addition, hostilities grow between the subcultures. Those who always lose cannot be expected to like those who seem to be lucky winners, often at the expense of the losers.[12]

If a strong corrective is applied, family scripts of poverty and failure do change. Dramatic evidence of this reversal is seen in many American Negro families who are all too often poor. With increasing legal and social pressure for affirmative action and under the influence of leaders who assert "Black is Beautiful" or "I'm Black and I'm Proud," failure scripts based on lack of opportunity and resulting low self-esteem are being rewritten toward self-respect and achievement. Potential losers are becoming potential winners.

family scripts and sex roles

Many family scripts have a set of strict directions for what men are supposed to be and do and for what women are supposed to be and do. It is not uncommon for a first-born son to hold a unique position within the family. He may be expected to carry on family traditions. He may be scripted to follow in his father's footsteps, doing the same kind of work or even going to work for him.

The second or third son may be thought of as a "baby," perhaps not as bright or as competent as an older brother. In other families the youngest boy — especially if he "looks like his daddy" — may receive all of dad's attention, while the first-born is given a less important role.

You may have wondered why two children, born of the same parents, can be so different. Aside from the different genes each child inherits, parents are at different places in their own emotional lives when each child is born.

Family scripting that determines masculine sex roles develops as a result of parents making frequent statements such as, "Men are to be the providers, it's not their job to do the housework." "It's up to the men to fix the car, paint the house, empty the garbage, and control the checkbook. That's what men are *supposed* to do!" The society at large reinforces stereotyping in schools, churches, business, job opportunities, and on TV.

Currently some different family scripting for men is emerging as a result of social pressure and changing economics. Often, when women work outside the home, the couple share household chores, financial responsibilities, and child rearing. This modeling is observed and copied. Eventually it will be part of the Parent ego state in the children. Also, increasingly, young men, using their Adult ego state, realize that society is modifying the definition of what was traditionally thought to be "women's work." A man now can begin to feel proud of being able to raise children and cook and keep house, instead of feeling ashamed for having these skills.

Sex role scripting can be firmly implanted in a very young child. Michele, a little girl of only three-and-a-half years old, revealed her role expectations in the following conversation with her mother.

> "I'm going to find a boy friend and marry with him. He'll go to the office and work and I'll stay home and take care of the babies, cause I got a breast to feed the babies.
>
> Mother: How about your going to the office and your husband staying home with the babies?
>
> Michele: 'Cause he can't do that. He is a Daddy and a Daddy can't stay home with the babies. I'll go to the office and help him some [Her mother does.] I get so tired waiting. I can't find a boy friend to marry with. I have to wait so long. Can I go on a date?
>
> Mother: What would you do on a date?.
>
> Michele: Walk around and hold hands and then come home and kiss."[13]

women's scripting   Women until recently have been scripted quite differently from men. The first-born female has often been expected to be "the little mother," performing household chores and taking care of younger brothers and sisters as part of her sexual role. Society, again, has reinforced this role in the same way it has reinforced men's roles.

In many families a girl is still cast in a "baby doll" role and is not expected to perform academically or vocationally. She may be scripted to be a cute, helpless sex object and as a result compete with other girls for the attention of the boys. TV soap operas used to cast women exclusively in stereotyped roles, and often still do.

Family scripting that determines feminine sex roles develops as a result of parents making frequent statements such as, "Don't bother with math. You'll never need it anyway," or "It's women's work to clean the house, cook the meals, and take care of the kids." Stereotyped feminine sex roles are perpetuated by copying behavior of other women, whether the behavior is appropriate to the present situation or not. Women need their Adult ego state to realize that they can change the script. Current research shows that many little girls are adapted to equate intellectual achievement and independence with loss of femininity. As a consequence, when such a woman uses her intelligence, she tends to belittle her successes and suffers from feelings of guilt over not being "womanly". She is going against her family scripting and social expectations and, without Adult understanding, her Child ego state has bad feelings about it. These feelings may persist even though she has every Adult reason to be proud of herself.

personal and sexual identity

Each of us learns to have feelings about our worth and talents as human beings — our *personal identity*. In addition, each of us also gathers feelings about being masculine or feminine — our *sexual identity*.

Sometimes we feel quite different about these two aspects of ourselves. For example, a young man might feel competent as a student and be well on his way to a successful vocation yet might also have learned to feel not-OK as a male. He may feel the need to "prove" himself over and over again by taking undue risks, by being tough, fighting, by being exceptional at a sport, or by collecting a lot of girlfriends.

In contrast, a young woman might learn to feel that she is pretty but that her intelligence and talents are not important or are an obstacle. Thus, she may feel OK about her feminine identity but not-OK about her unique abilities as a person. Whatever one's personal and sexual identity is, it will relate in some way to the expectations written into the family script and the larger cultural script.

People's sexual identity is expressed in the roles they play in adult life. The script is written in childhood when they fantasize, and maybe rehearse, what they'll do when they "get big" — playing house, playing school, doctor, nurse, cops and robbers, astronauts, and so forth. Most children are given toys that encourage them to follow certain sexual role expectations. These expectations, in turn, give a direction to their lives.

summary

In summary, some family scripts promote success, some promote failure. Some families rewrite their scripts by promoting change. However, in the life of any one individual, the most important forces in forming his or her script, including sex roles and sexual identity, are the messages sent by parent figures and the expectations of the culture and subculture.

exercises

1 evaluating case studies (group or individual)

Reread the case studies at the beginning of this unit (page 150) and discuss the following questions:

☐ Imagine Pat in his home. In what way might might his parents have acted toward him that affected his script?

☐ What roles do you think were acted out by Henrietta's mother and father?

☐ Draw an egogram of Henrietta. What was each of her ego states thinking and feeling?

☐ How do you think Bob felt about being a boy? What might he have said to himself about it?

☐ How did Bob's parents attitude affect his sexual identity?

☐ How might Charlene's script messages about being a girl affect her life at age 15, age 20, age 30, age 45?

2 stereotype phrases (individual and group)

Fill the following incomplete sentences with commonly heard words or phrases.

Girls are _____ because _____.

Women are _____ because _____.

Women are supposed to_____.

Boys are_____ because _____.

Men are _____ because _____.

Men are supposed to_____.

In small groups discuss the information or lack of information to back up the above statements.

3 male and female scripting messages (individual and group)

Look over the following list of words individually and supply typical messages children might receive about these subjects.

Subjects	Messages Given Girls	Messages Given Boys
Brains		
Physical appearance		
Vocation		
Education		
Achievement		
Money		
Masculine behavior		
Feminine behavior		

Now discuss the various messages in groups.

☐ Which of the messages seem to produce winners?

☐ Which produce losers?

☐ Does one sex tend to receive more positive messages than the other?

☐ What might be the long-term effect on boys or girls receiving these messages?

4 family and social scripting (group)

Discuss how some parents and relatives did or did not follow their family and /or social scripting in sex and job roles.

suggested research

1 family sex role interviews

Interview ten people asking the following questions:

☐ Who should do the dishes?

☐ Who should make household repairs?

☐ Who should decide on how money gets spent?

☐ Who should nurture the children?

☐ Who should discipline the children?

☐ Who should cook?

☐ Who should clean the home?

☐ Who should iron?

☐ Who should earn the money?

☐ Who should make the final decisions?

Keep a record and be prepared to take a class tally.

2 rating personal and sexual identity (journal entry)

I generally feel that:

I am not-OK _____ I am OK.
        −10   0   +10

I feel about myself as male or female:

I am not-OK _____ I am OK.
        −10   0   +10

☐ How can I improve my self-image?

My family generally feels that:

I am not-OK _____ I am OK.
        −10   0   +10

As a female (male):

I am not-OK _____ I am OK.
        −10   0   +10

☐ Do I need to discuss this with them?

☐ How do I go about it?

3 my identity

Raise these questions with yourself (perhaps for your journal): What does my family script mean to me personally? How has my identity been affected by it?

25 individual scripts

case study 1   Beth was the first child of young parents. She was born five weeks prematurely and had to spend the first weeks of her life in an incubator. He parents were like children themselves and had no experience with a baby that needed special care. When they brought Beth home from the hospital, they were worried about her but didn't know what to do, especially when she cried. Their pediatrician advised them to leave her alone to cry it out so she wouldn't be spoiled. Beth grew up underweight, nervous, and insecure. She shied away from people, and although she had several acquaintances, she had no close friends.

case study 2   Don was brought up as the youngest of a very large, wealthy family whose members all went their separate ways. His brothers and sisters were much older than he and he spent many days playing alone in his room, occasionally being checked on by a housekeeper. His contact with his parents was infrequent and rarely did they ever touch him, hold him, or play with him. When Don started first grade, he found it very difficult to be in a room with other children. When his teacher put her hand on his shoulder as she passed by his desk, Don would shrink away. As he continued in school, Don kept himself away from other students and would get "butterflies in his stomach" when in a crowd.

case study 3   Lucille was a cute baby, but her sixteen-year-old mother and eighteen-year-old father didn't want her. Each blamed the other for the pregnancy. "Why did you take advantage of me? Why did you lead me on and get me pregnant!" stormed the mother. "You should have taken care of yourself," stormed her father. They continually attacked each other with verbal abuse. They often hit Lucille when she cried, and yelled "Why don't you shut up!" Lucille grew up feeling she was no good and did not trust other people.

case study 4   John was the eagerly expected child of a second marriage. His father had not had children previously and was excited at becoming a father. His mother had two children by a previous marriage. She liked children, was in love with John's father, and was delighted with the prospect of a new baby. John was born when money was scarce, but his half-brother and half-sister took care of him, played with him, cuddled and admired him. His parents, when entertaining guests, proudly brought John out for approval. When alone, they laughingly bragged about their joint endeavor. John liked school and got along well with his classmates and most of his teachers. In fact, he eventually planned to be a teacher himself.

theatrical scripts and psychological scripts

Do you know people who seem very successful in their personal lives as well as in their school or work lives? Who have friends and vocational goals, who seem to know where they're going and how to get there, and who experience joy in the process of getting there? These people are living out constructive scripts.

Do you know people who are so despondent about life that they wish they had never been born? Do you have friends who work hard but for whom things never seem to come out right? Do you know people who get criticized a lot? People who are frequently getting into accidents or some other kind of trouble? People who continually complain or put down others? These people are living out destructive psychological scripts — destructive to themselves and/or to others.

Do you know people who seem to plod along in their work and their daily lives and never get very far? They like to keep things as they are and find it hard to change? They spend one day much like the day before? These people are living out a nonwinning or dead-end script.

Everyone has a psychological script. Psychological scripts, just like cultural scripts, are very similar to theatrical scripts. As individuals people act out their "parts" in life just as people play parts on the stage. They want certain scenery, wear costumes to present a certain character, use postures and gestures and tones of voice to indicate whether, at the moment, they are coming on as Victim or as Persecutor or as Rescuer, or if they are coming on straight.

Like a theatrical drama, each life has its own dramatic style. Some people live out a drama that might be called a saga, while others put on a comedy or a melodrama. Yet still others stage a farce or a tragedy. Most dramas that are acted on the stage have three acts.

Act I of a play introduces the setting where the action takes place, and the main characters — what they're like, how they come across, and their motives for what they do. In childhood, the first act of real life, character is formed. Children learn to feel OK or not-OK about aspects of themselves and others. They learn "favorite" feelings both negative and positive. They get used to a certain setting. They respond to these early life experiences by deciding who they are going to be, what they can do, and how they'll transact with other people.

Act II in a stage play deals with what happens to the main characters and what develops as a result of their specific situation and character. The inner and outer conflicts emerge. The plot thickens. In the second act of real life, people also act out their dramas according to the way their characters were formed. As the plots thicken, they too live out their inner and outer conflicts.

Act III in a drama portrays the resolution of the conflicts and problems that had been started in the first and developed in the second act. The resolution is how everything ends up, given the characters and the circumstances of the preceding acts. Every real life also has a final curtain. The person's psychological script largely determines what scene the curtain will finally fall on.

scripts and life plans

Eric Berne defines a psychological script as "an ongoing program, developed in early childhood under parental influence, which directs the individual's behavior in the most important aspects of his life.[14]

The script is like a blueprint for the shape one's life will take. It says what a person feels is "right" to do even if the plan is not well drawn. People follow their script compulsively. Sometimes the script differs from what actually happens to a person. New situations such as death, disease, disaster, and a determination to alter the script, can greatly change the course of an individual's personal history. However, a basic motivation that directs everyone's life is contained in the script.

Some people have a script that motivates them to realize their greatest potential. They receive messages that give them a basic confidence about themselves and their abilities. As a consequence they live according to *winning* script.

Other people may receive messages that cause them to live unsatisfying or very unhappy lives. They drudge along, being bored, unhappy, and make the same mistakes over and over. Their script goes nowhere. People with such scripts are very resistant to change. They are either fearful of new things and ideas, or they fear change will make them worse. Stuck in a rut, such people follow *nonwinning* or *going nowhere* scripts.

Still other people receive such negative messages that at best they end in failure, at worst in self-destruction. Such people follow *loser* scripts.

the scripting process

Act I, childhood, begins the scripting process. For example, a child who is ridiculed may decide, "I'm so clumsy, neither my parents nor anybody else will ever like me. I don't like myself." A child who is appreciated may decide, "I'm important, my family and others care about me. I like myself."

People use their life's time to act out a drama that proves what they decided as children. Each person, on the basis of experiences, figures out: Who am I? What can I do here? Who are all those other people? What will they do for me and I for them?

From the *specific* decisions they make about themselves and their family, children eventually take a more *general* position either that they're OK or that they're not-OK, that other people are OK or not-OK. Once these positions are taken, the person starts reinforcing these positions by what is called script-reinforcing behavior. Eventually, the stamps collected, the games played, the kinds of strokes given and received are all part of the script-reinforcing behavior. The script formula process goes like this:

CHILDHOOD EXPERIENCES ⟶ DECISIONS ⟶ POSITIONS ⟶ SCRIPT REINFORCING BEHAVIOR

(Being ridiculed for spilling things, falling down, making mistakes)   (I'm clumsy) (My parents will never like me)   (I'm not-OK) (They're OK)   (Doing clumsy things) (Getting ridiculed)

Scripting messages are received very early in life. Even an infant's experiences are part of a script. A child whose needs are met, who is fed, kept warm, rocked, and held, originally receives scripting messages of being lovable and wanted. Such messages are sent through sensations that feel good: Having an empty stomach filled, having wet cold diapers changed, having the touch of warm skin.

Contrast this with a child who is ignored and neglected; who perhaps goes hungry for long, long periods of time; who may lie wet and cold with nobody coming in response to cries of discomfort; who is left alone, rarely touched or cuddled. Or contrast this with an infant who is slapped or otherwise hurt for crying, for not finishing a bottle.

These experiences, even though they are mainly nonverbal, are perceived as scripting sensations. The young infant has no way to speak or to understand language but begins to *feel* important or worthless in response to the early care. The first script messages are received as physical sensations and become early script "tapes".

Later, infants begin to see things. They see facial expressions. They watch a parent's lips which are curling or bitter, a brow which is furrowed or straight, a face which responds warmly or rejects coldly. Infants first learn about the world they see, and thus they begin to gather additional feelings about others which reinforce feelings about themselves.

The words parents use to describe children when they speak *to* them or *about* them is another powerful way to shape scripts. "You're wonderful", "We love you," "I wish you'd never been born," "You're a nuisance" all shape a child's self-concept. Children who are described negatively by their parents will tend to describe themselves negatively.

Often the verbal messages sent by parent figures are sent through mottoes and sayings. Sometimes children "psych out" what the motto really means by "learning Martian."

mottoes and martian messages   Learning Martian is learning how to use intuition (the Little Professor) to find out where people really are. If you understand the meaning of the old cliche, "It's not what you say, it's the way you say it," then you understand Martian talk.

The Little Professor in the Child ego state is like someone who appears from Mars and who understands what people are *really* saying underneath the words they use. Sometimes what people are really saying matches their words; sometimes it doesn't.

Mottoes or favorite sayings are common scripting messages which many families use generation after generation. Each motto can have its Martian meanings.

For example, a common motto such as "The devil finds work for idle hands" could have a Martian's translation of "Keep working or you'll get into trouble". Or the motto "The way to a man's heart is through his stomach" can be translated "Be a good cook to get a man." Or the motto "Beauty is only skin-deep" could be translated "Good looks are not important" or "Don't be proud of your appearance" or "Don't be jealous of others who are better looking." Mottoes are interpreted differently by different Martians. Sometimes one parent uses one motto and another parent uses a conflicting one. The child who hears them is torn between contradictory messages.

All the experiences we have as children — early sensations of muscle tensions and relaxations, visual memories, words — are imprinted in our brains and nervous systems for most of our lives. Some children intuit their value by learning to understand Martian.

rehearsal and show time

During adolescence similar scenes to those in childhood may be acted out in a more sophisticated manner. These rehearsals are like rehearsals for the future drama. People begin to "try out" for parts they feel destined to play later — the parts their scripts dictate.

For example, in their current boyfriend-girlfriend scenes, they may rehearse their future marriages. Carolyn, who was bossy like her mother, had a boyfriend who was attracted to her for this quality. As a child he had decided, "I'm stupid so it's OK for other people to tell me what to do." When Carolyn told him what to do, he sometimes complained, "You're just like my mother." However, he still expected her to tell him what to do. Unless they both change, marriage or other close relationships for each of them are likely to have identical scenes to those rehearsed.

Phil was aggressively brutal like his father and always managed to have a girlfriend who in her childhood had been brutalized. Their relationship was a replay of earlier scenes and a rehearsal for future similar scenes to be developed more fully in Act II.

James had a different kind of rehearsal. He and his girlfriend had fun together, respected each other, and felt good about each other's successes. Their relationship was much like his mother and father's and would probably be replayed in similar ways in later life.

The kinds of scenes that Carolyn, Phil, and James each played out seemed to them to be the way things ought to be, whether full of pain or full of joy.

In Act II the show really goes on the road. This is likely to occur for most people during college years, or when they become self-supporting, get married, or make some other significant commitment to a way of life. The conflicts, problems, and successes which started in childhood are played out, but this time for keeps. It is during these years that a person's potential will be realized in some way, or neglected, or abused.

Act III starts for people at different ages..For many women it starts when the children are grown and leave home; for many men it starts when they get to the top in their job, or when they retire. This phase of life reveals how a person's relationships, accomplishments, and other important life events end up. How did the marriage work out? What happened to the children who were born? Where did the job lead to? What was life all about?

Every life comes to an end. This final scene is the finale to the ongoing life plan that may have been decided on in childhood. The show is over and only the audience response may be left.

exercises

1 evaluating case studies (group or individual)

Reread the case studies at the beginning of the unit (pp. 156-157) and answer the following questions for each of them:

☐ What might the person be like when he/she is in high school?

☐ What might the person be like 10 or 15 years after graduation?

2 scenes from a play in three acts (group)

Design a role playing situation of three *very brief* scenes.

1. A childhood scene where scripting occurs.

2. A high school scene where the same scripting shows.

3. A scene ten years later where the script is acted out.

3 mottoes and martians (group)

Discuss common mottoes that might be heard in families.

☐ What might the Martian meanings be?

☐ Do you think they'd mean the same things to different people?

☐ Which of these mottoes or meanings might be constructive and which defeating?

suggested research

1 imagining the future

Find a place where you can relax and be quiet for a few minutes. Read over the following questions and then close your eyes and think about them. You may want to think about just one question at a time. Write down your insights in your journal.

☐ What happens to people like me?

☐ If I go on as I now am, where will I end up?

☐ Who is really responsible for what I do with my life?

☐ Where do I plan to be and what do I plan to be doing when I'm:

20 years old

30 years old

40 years old

60 years old

80 years old

Check your answers again to make sure they are yours.

2 script check list

Role

The drama role I think I play most often is

_____.
Victim, Persecutor, Rescuer

People who know me well might think I
play the _____ role.

Theme

The theme of my drama could be
summarized in these words:

_____

The theme is similar to _____ in
character's name

_____.
fairytale, TV show, short story

Type of Script

The type of script I seem to be living out is
basically _____.
productive, destructive, going nowhere

If an audience were watching my life as if it
were a movie, they would feel _____.

If people in the audience talked about my
drama, they would say _____ ___.

Rewriting the Script

If I want to change my script I need to _____
instead of what I am now doing.

(You may want to enter some of your thoughts
and feelings in your journal.)

26 script roles and drama themes

case study 1   Carol was pregnant, no question about it, and too frightened to discuss it with anyone. Night after night she stayed awake, tossing and turning, wondering what to do. She couldn't make sense out of it. After all, her mother had continually told her, "You better be careful or you'll get pregnant too soon, just like I did." Her father had just as frequently said, "Girls like you can't be trusted to take care of themselves." Carol felt confused and inadequate. In her head she kept asking herself the question, "Why do things like this always happen to me?"

case study 2   Gordon, a senior, wasn't quite making it. His C-minus grades got him by, but that's all. "Every time I try something, it doesn't turn out bad, but it doesn't turn out good either," he lamented. "Sometimes I feel as if I'm treading water. I don't sink, but I don't get anywhere either. It's like when I was in the first grade, I tried and tried but couldn't read well. Other times I feel as if I have to keep running just to stay in the same place. Like a squirrel going around and around in the same place in the same cage." Gordon often added, "And look how hard I'm trying."

case study 3   Mr. Sudy was scheduled for a sabbatical leave. He planned on going back to school to get his master's degree in music and was excited and pleased over the prospect. Students in the band and choir had mixed feelings. They said they liked him and were glad he had the chance, but Mr. Sudy thought they looked depressed, as though he was deserting them, so he planned a farewell party. This was not a new experience for him. He had received the same praise and looks of loneliness when he started kindergarten, when he went off to Boy Scout camp, and when he received a scholarship at a college five hundred miles from home. Each time that Mr. Sudy moved on to a new experience, he was missed and cheered simultaneously.

stories and script themes   Have you ever seen someone living a life that seemed like a storybook tale? The lives of people often follow scripts that are similar to the lives heroes, heroines, and villians lead in mythology, fairy tales, folk lore, and popular radio and TV shows. Some people act out a part like Superman or Superwoman, leaping over tall buildings to rescue the less fortunate. Some people play the parts of the less fortunate, like the Poor Little Match Girl or the Little Lame Prince. Some people persecute and prey upon others like wicked witches and mean ogres.

Eric Berne says that children go around having experiences and one day they hear, read, or see a story that somehow fits their experiences. At this time they say, "That's me!" and identify with the characters and action. They may see themselves as a coward like the lion from the Wizard of Oz, as a wooden puppet like Pinocchio, as Cinderella victimized by a demanding family, as Mr. Spock from Star Trek, half man and half Vulcan, as a stumbling, bumbling fellow like Fred Flintstone, or as Peter Pan, never wanting to grow up.

Later in life they may choose friends expecting them to play predictable dramatic roles similar to those of their favorite childhood story. They may even identify with movies or plays which reflect these same types of characters and actions.

Cinderella is a script that is still commonly acted out today. A modern-day Cinderella may always be at the bottom of the class or get a menial job that is at the lowest level. She may see others as very demanding, as forcing her to do the dirty work. Cinderella is not interested in preparing herself for any kind of career because she holds the powerful delusion that someday she will meet her prince and be rescued from having to work at all. She spends much of her life just waiting, waiting for someone or something magical to happen. In a script rehearsal someone may lend her a dress so that she can go to a party in hopes of meeting her prince. Later in life she may still be waiting, working hard, getting an occasional new outfit, and looking for a prince year after year after year.

Sleeping Beauty and the Little Lame Prince

Sleeping Beauty holds a delusion similar to Cinderella's. A woman with a Sleeping Beauty script sets marriage as her only life goal. She does this to the exclusion of other ambitions and, consequently, does not develop her own unique talents and potentials. Instead she lies in a deep sleep in the sense that she does not take any difficult subjects in high school because she is "just going to get married." She does not continue her education. She does not even prepare herself to earn money. Sleeping Beauty, like Cinderella, expects a Prince Charming to come along and wake her up. In the meantime she may send out negative "vibes" that are, like the rose thicket, full of thorns. Her prince, if she finds one, will have to cut through these defenses.

Many American women have followed a Sleeping Beauty script. In the past, they could fill a lifetime with a script centered entirely around marriage and the family. Then the life expectancy of the average woman was 48 years. Her script didn't run out. She did.

Today's situation is quite different from what it was at the turn of the century. Modern woman has a life expectancy of 75 years. If her script runs out at age 40 -

45, when the children enter school or are grown and leave home, today's Sleeping Beauty experiences a sense of uselessness. It's much like, "Now that my story is over, there seems to be no purpose for me to live."

A similar script with a "waiting to be rescued" theme is that of the Frog Prince. He waits at the bottom of the pond for a princess who will be kind to him (perhaps at her parents' persuasion) and thereby break the spell so that he can become his handsome self once more. In real life, however, the Princess is likely always to see him as a frog, being very critical of his "froggy" behavior.

Another common script theme comes from the fairy tale of the Little Lame Prince who is banished to the tower by his royal parents because he is imperfect. In the tower a fairy godmother comes with a magic cloak that allows the Little Lame Prince to fly over No-Man's Land and see the trees and the grass for the first time. A modern-day Little Lame Prince is usually rejected by one or both of his parents as not being perfect. For example, he may not be athletic, or scholarly, or whatever his parents would like him to be. Though he receives adequate food and shelter, he does not receive the acceptance and love necessary to grow into a true prince. In a script rehearsal such a person, feeling "lame," is likely to seek some escape by "turning on" — perhaps through the magic cloak of drugs — thereby rejecting those who first rejected him.

Stories such as the ones above also contain script roles. The classic melodrama has a villain — the Persecutor; a hero — the Rescuer; and a heroine — the Victim. Persecutors are also often played by wicked witches, cruel stepmothers or stepfathers, and mean ogres. Greek mythology, too, is full of persecutors. Zeus, father of the Gods, controls others through reward, seduction, threat, and brutality. The goddess Athena persecutes heroes she's angry with and rescues those she likes.

Rescuers are often played by fairy godmothers, supermen or women, and perhaps people like Prometheus who in Greek mythology took fire from the gods and gave it to the mortals.

Victims are often played by Charlie Browns, wistful waifs, and captured maidens. Atlas in Greek mythology was destined to carry the burden of the world on his shoulders.

common script themes   Each person's psychological drama has a theme. A script theme runs like a thread through a person's life. It is expressed over and over and, in a sense, is the essence of a person's life story. For example, a common theme is "trying hard but never making it." People following this life theme invest lots of time in trying but may never get the job done, or the problem solved, or the decision made. They just keep trying and trying. One man who had this for his life theme said that his tombstone should read, "He tried and he tried, but finally he died."

Generally, script themes are expressed in short, crisp phrases. Each theme expresses a different bent to a person's life drama. Have you ever noticed people who are: Always Being Helpful, Bossing Others, Thinking Things Through, Getting Stepped On, Having New Ideas, Driving Others Crazy, Getting Out of Things, Getting Caught, Always On The Move? If so, you've seen them acting out their script themes.

Losing themes often show in the negative things people say over and over again. For example, people who frequently say things such as, "I'll never make it" or "Everything wrong always happens to me" or "I'm a born loser" are really verbalizing their script theme: failure. Such people *expect* things to go wrong, *expect* to be failures. And very often they are not aware that they are setting themselves up for such a life, consequently they are not aware that they can change it.

A *nonwinning theme* may show in such remarks made over and over again as "Let's not rock the boat" or "It's all I can do to stay even." This is verbalizing a script theme: going nowhere. People with this script do not *expect* to succeed or to fail. They do not expect change or development or progress. They are usually not aware that they are setting themselves up for near-failure. They have taken a middle-of-the-road position, always playing it safe.

A *winning theme* may show if positive remarks are frequently made. People who say "I feel good about myself and where I'm going with my life" or "I'm glad to be alive" or "Let's try again" are verbalizing a script theme — "I can do it." They expect to succeed in what they undertake and thus do not defeat themselves.

script themes and time

Sometimes the theme of a person's script reflects an element of time. For example, the word *after* may be said so often to some children — "Just wait until after your father comes home" — that they may conclude something bad will happen *after* they've had some fun. Constant comments such as "You can't trust people. They're always out to get you" may be translated, "After I make a friend, I can expect to get hurt." Or a lament such as "Just wait until *after* you're married, then you'll realize how hard it is to raise children," might be translated, "You can have fun now, but once you're married it's going to be misery and hard work." Many times, people with *after* themes in their scripts learn to expect something bad to follow something good. Berne writes of Damocles, a mythical Greek king who was happy but expected the worse to happen. Something was "hanging over his head." Many people have that feeling. In Damocles' case it was a sword suspended by a single horse-hair that hung over him. [15]

In contrast, people with *until* themes often learn to expect nothing good until they've done hard work or some difficult or unpleasant chore. This includes people who frequently hear, "You can't play *until* your work is done. They may translate this to mean that until the job is done they can't have fun. Many people who have *until* script themes feel that nothing good can happen while they work. For example, a student programed this way might delay enjoyment *until* all homework is finished and conclude that school work or work in general can never be enjoyable. Later in

168

life such people may select jobs they don't like because they've learned that nothing pleasant can occur *until* something unpleasant has happened. Hercules of Greek mythology was like this. He had to be a slave for 12 years before becoming a god.

People with *repetitive script themes* use their time doing the same thing over and over. Children may adapt this theme if frequently told, "Do it over and over until you do it right," and then observe their parents doing exactly that. The Greek Sisyphus had this theme. Forever, he rolled a big stone up a hill and just as he reached the top the stone would roll back and he would have to start all over.

One of the most common script themes related to time is the theme of waiting. People with *waiting themes* in their scripts often have chosen this because of frequently hearing such remarks as "Just wait and see. Everything will turn out all right" or "Everything comes to him who waits" or "Someday, the right person will come along." Such people are programed to live in the future waiting for a magical person or for their "ship to come in" to make their lives happier. They wait for someone else to rescue them from their feelings of boredom, loneliness, inadequacy, or from a bad situation. Mr. Micawber, in the novel *David Copperfield* by Charles Dickens, spent his entire life waiting, convinced that "something will turn up."

themes and roles *Waiting*: people who have script themes of waiting may be losers, nonwinners, or winners. They are into a loser script theme if they sit around and wait instead of doing something to solve their problems. Losers who are always waiting do not direct their own lives in any meaningful ways. Instead they expect someone else to do it for them.

The nonwinners with waiting themes are somewhat different. They don't expect other people to really solve their problems. Instead they make tentative efforts to do it themselves, but nonwinners procrastinate so much that they miss out on most opportunities. For example, nonwinners may delay signing up for classes that they want and therefore not get their favorite teacher. Or they may delay applying for a job and miss out getting it. They don't just sit and wait like a loser, they move just slowly enough to miss out on the best, always settling for second or third best.

Winners are different although they, too, wait. When winners wait, they do not wait passively to be rescued nor do they procrastinate. Instead they wait actively, gathering enough facts to make an intelligent decision, or preparing the next step until it's the appropriate time to make the right move. They also can postpone an immediate gratification for a long-term goal and more intense strokes.

Hoping: A script theme of hoping can be looked at in the same way. Losers are those who hope for pie in the sky or for Santa Claus to bring something for nothing. They hope that their ship will come in, that the right person will come along, that a new car will give them what they want out of life, that opportunity is just around the corner. But such people never bother getting to the corner, nor do they prepare to meet their ship.

Nonwinners hope for a little success; they try, but not much. They may hope for an adequate job, may hope for a so-so boyfriend or girlfriend, may hope for passing grades. Because nonwinners only hope for a little success, they never get the real thing.

Winners also hope, but they hope for real success. They take action and make plans to achieve it. They may hope to get a part in a school play for which they've worked. They may hope to take a trip for which they've saved money. They may hope to go to college having taken courses and gotten grades that make it possible.

Trying: A script theme of trying can also be looked at this way. Losers try to get their homework done but then are "too tired," may try to get a job but are "too afraid," may try to get a friend but are sure no one would want to be one. They make the same trying mistakes over and over again.

Nonwinners who have trying script themes try to get their homework done and get some of it done, try to get a job but not the one they really want, try to get a friend but pick out people who don't want to be very friendly.

Winners who try achieve their goals. They don't keep doing things that don't work. If one method doesn't work they try another. They try to get their homework done and plan their time so they do. They try to get a job, even when they're afraid, and keep trying until they do. They try to find a friend, plan how to do it and end up with several. They experiment and practice until they get the desired results.

exercises

1 evaluating case studies (group or individual)

Reread the case studies at the beginning of the unit (page 165) and answer the following questions:

☐ What is the theme of Carol's script?

☐ What might she be like in five years? In ten years? In twenty years?

☐ What is the theme of Gordon's script?

☐ What was the theme of Mr. Sudy's script?

☐ How would his position affect his script?

2 updating old stories (group)

Select some fairy tales or childhood stories that were not discussed in this unit.

☐ Figure out how the story themes could be acted out. For example, if people are into a Robinson Crusoe script, what might they do? If they were into Huck Finn or Tom Sawyer scripts, what kind of grownups might they be? How would Dr. Zhivago be played in a contemporary setting?

3 your script theme in three styles (individual)

If you are beginning to get in touch with your own script theme, write it out in all three ways. How would you act it out as:

A loser   a non-winner   a winner

suggested research

1 research on drama themes

Check *TV Guide* or newspaper ads for titles of shows and movies:

☐ What kinds of TV shows or movies seem to be most popular?

☐ Do they have basic common themes, such as violence, illness, love, adventure, the supernatural, or what?

☐ Write a one-sentence line that summarizes the theme of five movies or TV shows.

2 time themes and scripts

Write out thumbnail sketches of yourself and two other people who are close to you. These should be brief, only a few sentences. You may want to consider the epitaph for each of you.
After writing, think over these questions:

☐ What key word does your sketch suggest such as "after", "waiting", "hoping", "until", or whatever you see?

☐ Does the life sketch seem to be that of a winner, or a loser, or a nonwinner, or some combination?

☐ What could be changed in each thumbnail sketch to strengthen the person's "winning streak"?

part six

27 time structuring

case study 1 Sylvia was often spoken of as the "quietest girl in the school." She would scurry down the hall looking neither right nor left, speaking only if spoken to and then only with a brief nod or "Hello." Although she kept mostly to herself, she occasionally spent some time talking to her neighborhood friend, Barbara. When Barbara's mother asked her, "What in the world were you and Sylvia talking about, standing out on the street for so long?" Barbara would look puzzled and respond, "I really don't know. We just talked about a lot of things but really didn't talk about anything!"

case study 2 Herb, Sylvia's brother, was frequently called "the school's biggest troublemaker." Time and time again he would do things that ended up getting him suspended or getting a low or failing grade. Herb walked with an air of bravado, and the list of four-letter words he often used was extensive. On the surface he gave off a belligerent message of "Just try and make me do it." Herb headed a gang whose members dressed alike and held secret meetings. When anything went wrong they always felt it was someone else's fault and that other people were out to get them.

case study 3 Bessie limped when she walked, because she'd had polio as a child. She was easy to be around, seldom complained and had many friends. Bessie always seemed to see the best in everyone. Even crabby old Mrs. Dilworth down the street smiled when Bessie stopped for a minute to say hello to her. Bessie really cared about people and often took time for them, even though she was very busy with school projects, her guitar lessons and her ceramics classes.

People structure their time in different ways. Favorite ways of structuring time can come from any ego state. In their Parent ego people will use time as their parents did. In their Adult they will use time logically. In their Child they may use time as an expression of their Natural Child, their Little Professor, or their Adapted Child. For example, *withdrawal* is a way of structuring time that is often an adaptive pattern from early childhood. Many children cope with uncomfortable situations by pulling away from others, by isolating themselves, by not paying attention to what's going on.

withdrawal Withdrawal can be physical or emotional. People withdraw *physically* from others when they avoid a discussion to go for a walk alone or go into a room and close the door. Some withdraw *emotionally* by just pulling into their own heads, letting their minds go blank or engaging in fantasies of "What if I were with someone else" or "If only I had a million dollars." Or they may daydream about something special they want to do someday or someplace they want to be. Or they may hide out in front of a TV screen or behind a book. Whenever people withdraw either physically or psychologically, they separate themselves from whomever they're with for a period of time.

    Withdrawal can be positive or negative. All people need some time for themselves. It is a positive withdrawal when one takes time to think; time to be aware of one's fantasies and dreams; time to experience the sensations of sun and sand, and sounds and scents; lying on one's back watching the clouds or listening to the wind blowing through the pines while letting one's imagination take flight. This withdrawal can be positive rest and recreation or a time for introspection and planning. Withdrawal is negative when people sulk and indulge themselves by wallowing in negative feelings of loneliness, self-pity, hostility, or resentment.

rituals People use some of their time to go through what are called *rituals*. Rituals are stereotyped series of transactions that are highly predictable. Saying "Hello" and getting a "Hello" back is a two-stroke ritual. "How are you?" "Fine" is another two-stroke ritual. The most common rituals of any culture are those of greeting. Whereas in America many people feel comfortable with just saying "Hi," greeting rituals in other cultures are more formal and perhaps more lengthy. Rituals are predictable ways of relating to other people.

    Many rituals are centered around family life, national traditions, holidays, religious beliefs, etc. Some of them add order and predictability to people's lives; some hold deep meaning as, for example, certain religious rituals or the ritual of getting married. However, if a whole life is primarily patterned by ritualistic living, growth and development of people are inhibited because they don't risk new creative ways of thinking, feeling, and behaving.

pastimes *Pastiming,* another common way of spending time, often follows a ritualistic greeting. When pastiming, people simply talk to one another about subjects that are of little consequence. One of the most common pastimes that people engage in is centered around the topic of the weather. "Gee, it sure is hot." "Yeah, summer's coming," or "Gee, it sure is cold." "Maybe it's going to snow tonight." Any subject can be used as a pastime—cars, friends, current records, TV shows, etc. Pastimes are sometimes a waste of time. For example, nothing productive may come out of an exchange about the weather.

One common pastime is *Ain't It Awful*. Most lunch periods are filled with at least some talk about how awful something or someone is, without any suggestions of what could be done about it. The reverse of this is *Ain't It Wonderful*. After a successful play has been staged, actors as well as audience often pass some time lauding, "Wasn't it wonderful!"

During pastimes people may become aquainted with each other and perhaps begin to learn what interests they have that might lead them into a deeper relationship. However, people who stay at a pastime level never get to know one another really well.

games
Pastimes often lead to *psychological games*. Games tend to be an unproductive use of time, since they are played to avoid doing anything else like solving a problem, making a decision, getting close to people.

Games result in bad feelings because people play games to get and to give negative strokes without knowing it. Structuring time with games often indicates that the players are involved in feelings of the past and are reinforcing their negative positions and feelings rather than being involved in what's going on right now.

activities
A fifth way people structure time is by *engaging in activities*. Activities are what is commonly called work—getting something done, getting something accomplished. People who work on a project together, who play on a team or in a band together, who cook a meal together or repair a car or do homework are all involved in activities. Many of the activities that people engage in during a day are related to their jobs, their education, or their hobbies.

Generally speaking, activities are useful and rewarding ways to spend time. However, a life that is exclusively made up of activities, especially solitary activities, may be somewhat sterile, devoid of social courtesies and friendly laughter.

intimacy
Sometimes people experience authentic intimacy. The word *intimacy* is often understood to mean infatuations or sexual relations. This is not an accurate use of the word. Many sexual contacts that are made in the back seat of a car at a drive-in movie or an isolated parking spot have little to do with genuine intimacy. Indeed, in some cases it may be exploitation rather than real caring that brings about such contacts.

Intimacy implies an open relationship with no ulterior transactions. It is game-free. During moments of intimacy people do not try to get anything out of each other. They are not possessive or demanding. They are simply being with one another, listening to one another, and caring about one another. At such times people feel appreciative, tender, and affectionate. These feelings may be expressed through joyful laughter, caring gestures, or peaceful silence.

Intimacy may be uncomfortable, particularly for those people who are adapted to be fearful and distrustful of others, to keep their distance, to avoid closeness. These people unknowingly choose games, rituals, or pastimes as a way of avoiding being real or being too emotionally close to other people.

However, the activities people share and the moments of intimacy they experience together are the most positive ways of structuring time to give and get winning strokes.

scripts and time structuring

People who spend much of their lives with rituals, pastimes, and withdrawal patterns live out scripts that are neither destructive nor constructive. Such people often feel bored with themselves and with life in general. They lack a zest for living and are frequently boring to be around. They either withdraw psychologically and are therefore not really present, or they transact at such a superficial level that nothing authentic ever happens between them and other people. They are unwilling or afraid of being open, and therefore miss out on the closeness that winners can experience.

People who spend much of their time playing psychological games are living out destructive scripts. They are spoiling their own lives and the lives of others. Their scripts are like B movies, like melodramas that are soon forgotten, disliked, or avoided. Their time may be structured with excitement, but ultimately it is destructive.

People who spend much of their time engaged in activities and intimacy are likely to be living out constructive scripts. They are going somewhere with their lives and know it. They are interested and interesting to be around. They may have a zest and healthy excitement for life. Although they may occasionally play games, they break them up whenever possible. They use withdrawal, rituals, and pastimes only where appropriate, not as a way of killing time, filling time, or wasting time. People who structure their time with intimacy know how precious life and people really are.

time structuring in friendship and marriage

In meaningful friendships, the people usually structure their time around activities of common interest. They do not always feel close and intimate. These feelings ebb and flow like the tides.

Real friendships—like good marriages—last because of a basic trust, because of a basic willingness to be real and to let the other person also be real. There is a sense of responsible caring without exploitation. Real friends help each other grow and avoid playing phoney roles and putting on manipulative acts.

Friends structure their time playing together, laughing at each other's jokes, crying over each other's grief. They structure their time together with activities, planning a joint venture, working toward a common goal. They also structure their time caring about each other, helping out when things get tough.

In a marriage where the two people involved are close and really like each other, each feels empathy towards the other, yet at the same time lets the other person "just be." Neither acts as master or slave, as owner or object to be possessed. Though friends or spouses may be separated by time or distance, each feels a sense of loyalty and both are glad to be with each other when next they meet.

the merry-go-round of time

It has been stated that life for some people is like a merry-go-round with the horses going up and down, the people going round and round, and the ring they reach for turning out to be only brass. And that is how some people spend their lives—going round and round in endless rituals, pastimes, and games, withdrawing from the real world of satisfying activities and intimacy.[16]

A play that was popular around 1970 was called "Stop the World, I Want to Get Off." One of the songs in it, "What Kind of Fool Am I?" is the lament of a man who is financially successful but never falls in love. Life for him is devoid of authentic intimacy.

summary

In summary, many people ask themselves, "What shall I do with my life?" This question is always related to, "What shall I do with my time?" Put another way, "What are my goals?" is related to "Am I using my time in the best way to achieve my goals?" These questions are of life-long significance. There are no easy answers. What people do with their lives and their time are value decisions. The value they place on the needs of their Child, the activities of their Adult, and the traditions of their Parent, largely determines their life goals and the way they structure time to achieve them.

178

exercises

1 evaluating case studies

Reread the case studies at the beginning of the unit (page 174) and explore the following possibilities:

- ☐ How did Sylvia structure her time at school and with her friend Barbara?

- ☐ Why did she use this method?

- ☐ How did she seem to structure her time with her friend, Barbara?

- ☐ How might this affect their relationship?

- ☐ What was Herb's favorite way of structuring his time and how was it related to his life's script?

- ☐ How did his gang structure their time together?

- ☐ How did Bessie structure her time with the neighbor lady?

- ☐ What were other ways she used her time?

2 ego states and time structuring (group)

Discuss which ego states are most likely to be involved when structuring time in each of the six ways listed below. Also discuss the negative and the positive possibilities of such structuring.

Ways of Structuring Time   Ego States Involved

Withdrawal

Rituals

Pastimes

Games

Activities

Intimacy

3 time collage (individual or group)

Collect or draw pictures of people structuring their time in the six different ways we have discussed. Paste them on large sheets of paper, lable them, and put them up on the walls. Have an informal art show and discuss whether or not there is class agreement on how the pictures are labeled.

4 identifying time structuring (group)

Make a list of 12 or more things that people said and did in your group during the last exercise. For each item, determine how time was structured.

	Activity	Time Structure
sample:	Ann cut out pictures for collage	said or did
	Jim cracked a joke	pastime

suggested research

1 time awareness

Observe closely for a few days the many ways people speak about time. Do they say they waste it? Use it? Kill it?

- ☐ Make a list of common expressions about time. Figure out how the comments fit into one of the categories of time structuring and the type of script that the comments may hint at.

- ☐ Then make a table like the one on the next page and fill it in.

2 your ego states and your time

For each ego state determine your thoughts and feelings that are related to the subject of time. For example, your Parent may be programed, "A stitch in time saves nine," or "Don't waste time," or "Time is precious."

ego states	thoughts, feelings, and messages
P	
A	
C	

Now ask yourself, "Which of these messages, thoughts, and feelings do I really want to follow in my own life planning? What do I really value when I think about it?"

Common comments about time	Type of time structuring	Type of script indicated: constructive, destructive, going nowhere

28 contracts for winning

case study 1 Jeannie studied hard and got good grades. She also held a part-time job at a hamburger stand where she was allowed to eat all the hamburgers and french fries that she wanted without cost. Consequently, Jeannie was overweight. Another trait of hers was to put all the money she earned into a savings account, seldom buying clothes, going to movies, or doing anything that would cost money. When Jeannie was younger, her parents had been very poor. Hunger had been a reality then. However, as she grew older and her parents had better jobs, hunger was no longer a threat. As Jeannie studied TA she found out why she was so miserly and often unattractive. She made a decision not to overeat because of an old childhood fear and to spend some money on herself every week.

case study 2 Neil was on probation for cutting classes, hot-rodding a car, and breaking into a pet store, robbing the till. Neil was bright enough but structured his time like a loser. The games he played with authority figures inevitably led to his getting some kind of psychological kick. His probation officer had told him that the next time he broke the rules he might be sent to an institution. One day when thinking about his future life, Neil decided to change the direction in which he was going. He believed he could choose a better way to spend his time than doing time in prison.

case study 3 Lynn and Pablo had gone steady since they were juniors in high school. In their relationship Pablo was always putting Lynn down and bossing her around. While she complained in a whiney voice that she didn't like it, she seemed to accept it. Through better understanding of their ego states and of their scripts, they began to talk over this part of their relationship. Pablo agreed that he would stop discounting Lynn and that he would be less bossy. Lynn agreed that she would stop playing the part of the whiney complainer and that when she *felt* discounted or pushed around, they would talk it over, discover what was happening between them, and straighten it out. They decided that if they couldn't straighten things out it was not a winning relationship.

introduction to contracts

Most people have things they'd like to change about themselves. In TA the way to go about it is to make a *contract*. A contract then becomes an effective tool for change.

A contract for change is a *specific goal* that a person decides to accomplish and *a carefully thought out plan to reach that goal*. It is an Adult commitment to one's self and/or to someone else to make a change. Usually contracts are a move away from the negative aspects in one's life to establishing more positive aspects.

The contract must be clear, concise, and direct. It involves:

1. a decision to work on a specific problem.
2. a statement of the precise goal to be reached, put in language that is simple enough for the inner Child to understand.
3. the possibility of the goal's being fulfilled; it must be realistic.

In order to make contracts, people need to have enough awareness of their approach to life to know what is causing them or others dissatisfaction or undue discomfort. This means getting in touch with their scripts and their not-OK feelings. Dissatisfaction often motivates change.

It is important that a contract be made by the Adult ego state. If a person had a parent figure who put him or her off by making promises and then not keeping them, that person's Parent ego state may be programed to use promises as put-offs, or that person may make a "New Year's Resolution" from the Child ego state with no honest intention of keeping it. Good intentions that are not acted on don't bring about change. The Adult plays it straight, knows what needs changing, and sets about doing it.

types of contracts

Contracts are usually made around solving problems. The problem that needs solving can involve behavioral change, attitudinal change, or a change in mental and physical health.

Contracts involving *behavioral change* could be made, for example, if the problem is a bad temper, procrastination, alcoholism, or drugs. People can *decide* to change such behavior patterns and accomplish it by using their Adult.

Contracts involving *attitudinal change* could be made, for example, by people who feel they are so ugly no one would like them, or those who feel like losers and lowest on the totem pole, or stupid and unable to succeed, or insecure about their masculinity or femininity.

Contracts involving *health* could be made by people who smoke, or who seldom go for a physical checkup when something is wrong, or who say they need to lose (or gain) weight but never actually do it.

Many contracts overlap each one of the above categories. When first learning to make contracts, it's best for people to start with something small they want to change. Gradually they learn how to make larger contracts because they will be building on their own successes. It's always easier to begin learning mountain climbing on a foothill than to start with Mt. Everest.

goals and contracts Many people avoid setting goals because they are afraid of failure. Yet winners learn from their mistakes as well as from their successes. Winners avoid failure if they can, but they don't avoid taking action for fear something might fail. Just as scientists, for example, often have many failures before their experiments turn out right, writers usually have to rewrite their material many times before it says what they want it to say. When learning how to dance, or ride a bike, or sew a shirt, or fix a car, the mistakes often precede the successes. This is as true for children learning to play as it is for students learning to think, and for people of any age learning how to live.

Setting a goal is one key to effective living and there are many ways to set goals. Some people list all the things they want, then number them according to importance. The order they choose depends on what they value. Other people take a goal a day and focus on that one thing. Still others wait for a flash of inspiration or insight, then decide how to work on that. Your way may be uniquely yours and successful. If you have a fear of failure it is probably related to a dependency pattern. You may be oversensitive to the approval or disapproval of others.

If so, begin to think of criticism as *useful feedback* which you can evaluate with your Adult ego state and accept or reject. Granted, your Child may want total acceptance from others and your Parent may want you to be 100 percent perfect, but it is your Adult that is meant to be and can be the executive of your personality. There is always something to be learned from every criticism and your Adult will evaluate whether others are right or wrong.

If you set goals and establish contracts to reach these goals, and if the goals and contracts are met with criticism, stop, count to ten and ask yourself, "I wonder if by any chance this could be correct." Think about it for a while, then ask yourself, "I wonder if by any chance this could be incorrect." You may need to listen to your own thoughts to get more data before you decide.

A useful body technique for immediate change or decontamination is the *Adult leveling position.* It is used by people who wish to think clearly about their goals and contracts. It activates their Adult to organize facts and materials from an objective position, not from a subjective or prejudicial position. The Adult leveling position is taken by sitting upright (not rigid) in a straight chair, feet flat on the floor, arms or hands uncrossed, letting them hang down loosely, or resting comfortably, chin parallel to the floor. It is important not to tip the head either right or left, and to look straight ahead. This is a "coming on straight" position in which it is almost impossible to feel negative or confused. It is an important aid for clear thinking. People have a right to respect their own thinking as well as the thinking of others.

noncontract and contract phrases

When specifying contracts people need to listen carefully to the words they use. Many words and phrases do not show commitment to achieving their goals.

"I'd *like* to change" is a noncontract phrase. Nothing will happen. A contract phrase would be, "I'm going to change . . ." (naming a specific thing.)

"I think I might . . ." is a noncontract phrase. A contract phrase would be, "I've thought about it and it will . . . ."

"I'd like to explore . . ." is a noncontract phrase unless it's followed by specifics such as, "I'd like to explore various vocations and I will do it by. . . ."

When making valid contracts, the first step is a *clear statement of a goal,* preferably in writing. Common contract phrases are "I am going to stop _____ and instead _____" or "The problem I need to solve is _____" or "The question I need to find an answer to is _____."

The second step is the *plan of action.* To develop this, ask the question, "What am I *willing* to do to reach my goal?" or "What will I need to do? When? Where? How?"

The third step involves a *plan for evaluation* by using the questions: "How will I know when I've reached my goal?" "How will other people know?"

The fourth step involves *awareness of games* either played with oneself or with others. The questions to be asked are, "What do I do to sabotage myself?" "How do I undermine myself?"

Many people have goals but are not willing to put in the time and effort necessary to achieve the goals. Ask yourself, "What am I *willing* to do for me?"

contracts and discounts

Some people do not become the winners they could be because they discount the problem.[17]

1. They do not take it seriously
2. They claim it's not that important
3. They claim nothing can be done about it
4. They claim they themselves can't do anything about it

For example, if given a homework project they may not pay attention to the assignment (not take it seriously), or not do it ("it's not important"), or say nobody could figure it out ("nothing can be done about it"), or give up on it ("I just can't do it").

Discounting problems is often a habit of long standing. Such habits are not changed by wishing and wanting but by deciding and acting.

the secret of good contracts

These four words are important as a technique for firming up a contract—wish, want, decide, and act.

When people just *wish* for some goal, they only daydream about it and do nothing. When people *want* some goal, they make tentative attempts to reach it which could lead to decisions but usually lead to giving up just before they succeed. When people finally *decide* on some goal, they make plans on how to achieve it. These plans are then carried out by action steps.

Wishers and wanters are like boats cast adrift on an ocean without a rudder or a captain. Deciders are like boats being steered by a competent captain who uses a compass, and is headed toward a precicely marked destination. To reach this destination there must be a chart that is followed.

Wishers and wanters overuse the Child ego state waiting for a Rescuer or a Santa Claus. Deciders use the Adult and set contracts for winning.

exercises

1 evaluating case studies (group or individual)

Reread the case studies at the beginning of this unit (page 181) and consider the following questions for each case:

☐ What was the decision made?

☐ What words might have been used to establish the contracts?

☐ What could be a winning plan of action?

2 dear abby (group or individual)

Bring copies of "Dear Abby" or similar columnists who give advice in a newspaper. Each person select one problem, read it aloud, then discuss how the following blanks could be filled in:

☐ If I were to answer that person's letter, I would tell him/her to _____.

☐ My response is likely to come from my _____ ego state.

☐ The ego state from which the person seems to have written for advice is _____.

☐ A possible contract for that person could be _____

3 music and problem solving (group)

Bring a popular singer's record to school. Play a part of it for the class and describe which ego state the lyrics imply and which ego state the lyrics are trying to hook. Then consider the following questions.

☐ What problem is being described in the song?

☐ Do the words encourage the listener to do certain things or think certain ways?

☐ Is anything being done to solve the problem?

☐ With that problem, what could be some of the options?

☐ What kinds of contracts might be needed?

4 the current you (individual)

☐ List 20 words that describe you in relation to your family.

☐ List 20 words that describe you in relation to your school.

☐ List 20 words that describe you in relation to your personal goals.

☐ After you have made your list, put a W for winner, an NW for nonwinner, or an L for loser after each one of the words. Is there anything you can do to improve the NW or L descriptions?

suggested research

1 before and after brochure

Make up a booklet telling about yourself. Label Part I of the booklet "Before" (before you learned about TA) and Part II "After" (after you learned TA). Include some drawings in your brochure.

☐ Use any kind of materials you like — newspaper or magazine ads, pieces of colored paper, words that you write yourself or cut out from some place. Be as creative as you like, but let this advertise you, before and after.

2 life goals and contracts for a journal

Asking yourself specific questions will lead you to contracts that will help you achieve your life goals. Ask yourself:

1. What are my life goals?

☐ Make a list of your life goals, taking no more than two minutes. Try to get down as many words as you can during that brief time. List anything that comes into your head, even far-out ideas.

2. What do I want to do with the next year?

☐ Again list your answers as quickly as you can for two minutes.

Now study your lists, then continue self-questioning.

3. What would be the best use of my time right now so that I can move toward fulfilling my goal?

4. What would I need to do differently instead of what I now do?

5. Am I willing to do it?

6. Beginning when?

7. How will I know when I've achieved it?

8. How would others know?

9. How might I sabotage myself?

10. What can I decide to do so as not to sabotage myself?

2 winning contracts

☐ Sit in a comfortable place and project an imaginary film that will show what you would like to be doing and how you would like to feel in one year.

☐ Next ask yourself what you would need to do with your time to get there.

☐ List three specific things you could change.

☐ Set a date for when you will start each step.

☐ Set dates for completion.

☐ Now think about:

What do I *wish* for?

What do I *want*?

What have I *decided*?

What will I *do* about it?

29 getting it all together

The only two reasons for this unit are to let you firm up your contracts by sharing them with others, and to have fun with what you've learned in TA.

sharing contracts

If you have decided to change a pattern, get together with another person who also has decided to work on something.*

1. Share your contracts.

2. Plan to check with each other in two weeks to see how you're both doing on the contracts and if they need to be reevaluated or restated. (Look over the guides in Unit 28 for stating a good contract.)

3. Make another plan to get together a month from now and share what successes you've had making your change.

4. Don't be afraid to brag a little.

*If you haven't decided to make any changes, get together with someone and discuss why not.

having fun with contracts

Blow up balloons. Select your favorite color if you can. With a felt pen write on the balloon some feeling or attitude or habit you want to get rid of. When everyone is ready, let the balloons fly or pop them.

Now blow up another balloon and write something on it that is important to you and your goals — like a motto or saying or a good feeling.

You might want to tie this one up with a string and keep it for a while. It will help you continue your winning ways.

evaluating your experience with the people book

Make a drawing like the one shown below and state your opinions, thoughts, and feelings about transactional analysis.

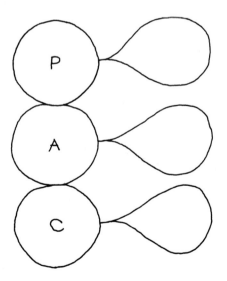

footnotes

1. George R. Metcalk, *Black Profiles* (New York: McGraw-Hill, 1968) p. 7.

2. Dee Brown, *Bury My Heart at Wounded Knee* (New York: Bantam Books, 1973). pp. 176-189.

3. Clarke Newlon, *Famous Mexican-Americans* (New York: Dodd Mead, 1972), pp. 50-69. Quotations from pp. 53-54.

4. Eric Berne, M.D., *Transactional Analysis in Psychotherapy* (New York: Grove Press, 1961), p. 33.

5. Thanks to John Dusay, M.D., for the egogram concept.

6. Claude M. Steiner, *Games Alcoholics Play: The Analysis of Life Scripts* (New York: Grove Press, 1971).

7. Eric Berne, M.D., *Principles of Group Treatment* (New York: Oxford University Press, 1966), pp. 286-288.

8. Thanks to Stephen Karpman, M.D., for the triangle concept.

9. Eric Berne, M.D., *What Do You Say After You Say Hello?* (New York: Grove Press, 1973), p. 24.

10. John James, "The Game Plan", *Transactional Analysis Journal* (Vol. 3, No. 4, Oct. 1973), pp. 14-17.

11. Peter I. Rose, *They and We: Racial and Ethnic Relations in the United States* (New York: Random House, 1964), pp. 102-112.

12. Thomas Szasz, *The Myth of Mental Illness* (New York: Dell Publishing, 1961), p. 230.

13. Paschal Baute, Unpublished paper, 1973.

14. Berne, *What Do You Say After You Say Hello?*, p. 418.

15. *Ibid.*, p. 206.

16. Thanks to John Fugit for this metaphor.

17. Jacqui Lee Schiff with Beth Day, *All My Children* (New York: M. Evans, distributed in association with J.B. Lippincott, 1971), pp. 210-211.

The first three case studies in Chapter 1 were adapted from *Cradles of Eminence* by Victor and Mildred Goertzel (Little Brown, 1962).

acknowledgments

Frank Costello: all photos except those listed below.

Dave Brigham: 2 bottom left, 18 top left, 19 top right, 143 bottom right, 173 bottom right.

Terry Watters: 2 top right, 2 bottom right, 3 bottom left, 142 top left, 143 top right.

Marty Viljamaa: cartoons.

190

index